What People Are Saying About *Emotionally Intelligent Leadership*

"Leadership can be learned, but does take some work . . . Taking the time to read, follow, and use this book can only lead to a deeper understanding of who we are and how we can make an impact in the world. I wish I had this when I was a student."—*Paul Pyrz, president, LeaderShape, Inc.*

"This well-organized and easy-to-read guide covers core leadership development concepts in a way that is relevant and applicable for students."—*Kelly Hannum, research scientist, Center for Creative Leadership*

"Shankman and Allen have written an intriguing book that can be of real value to college student leaders and the professionals who advise them. 'Emotionally intelligent leadership' is not just a cute phrase they have invented; it is a thoughtful concept that emerged from their scholarly analysis and extensive experience. Helping college students develop into good leaders is a special challenge, and this book is an important contribution to the field."—*Art Sandeen, retired vice president for student affairs, University of Florida*

"*Emotionally Intelligent Leadership* synthesizes what is known about effective leadership and places it in the context of the lives of today's college students. It is easy to read and provides a helpful handbook for college students who want to work intentionally to improve their leadership ability. The book offers questions to stimulate reflection, practical examples to improve understanding of the concepts presented, and useful suggestions for applying the ideas offered. The many quotes from college student leaders help give the book a real-world feel."—*Richard McKaig, vice president for student affairs, Indiana University*

"*Emotionally Intelligent Leadership* is an exciting and provocative read. Leadership books for college students are few and far between; this one is definitely a keeper. The combination of theory with practice and real student stories makes *Emotionally Intelligent Leadership* an excellent addition to any leadership collection."—*Les Cook, vice-president for student affairs, Michigan Technological University*

"This is a great primer for all who wish to be authentic leaders in an ever-changing world."—*Jonathan Brant, director, Beta Theta Pi Foundation*

"This book is a terrific leadership development resource for students. Unlike other books in its genre, this resource is explicitly grounded in the literature and links theory to practice."—*Tiffany Hansbrough, director, David Brain Leadership Program, Baldwin-Wallace College*

"Finally a book delivers a tailored approach to developing leadership potential. Meeting student potential where it is at, providing them with the necessary tools they need, and taking them where they need to go—a win-win read."—*David Rae, project manager, University of Oregon Leadership Summit*

"The emotionally intelligent leadership model and overall style of this book will provide college students with a valuable personal resource for leadership development that is otherwise largely absent from popular leadership literature."—*Kevin Arnold, assistant director for leadership programs, Kravis Leadership Institute, Claremont McKenna College*

"[A]n accessible read for students interested in developing a better understanding of their own leadership potential. The real-world examples, brevity of chapters, and inclusion of student quotes provide a valuable and identifiable road map, while the focus on emotionally intelligent leadership teaches students to reflect on their passions, actions, and life journey."—*Sean Creighton, executive director, Southwestern Ohio Council for Higher Education*

"Marcy and Scott present a passionate, practical and innovative approach to understanding how intellect and emotions propel our ability to be effective leaders. This book is an excellent contribution to the literature on teaching students leadership competence and organizational culture and is required reading for those seeking self-knowledge, harmony, and balance in relationships."—*Sentwali Bakari, dean of students, Drake University*

"With its focus on emotional intelligence, this book adds to our understanding of leadership. Students will see themselves in the voices and examples that are used and will find the reflection questions helpful in exploring their inner leader."—*Tim McMahon, faculty development, University of Oregon; coauthor,* Exploring Leadership

"Using easily recognizable examples and simple yet articulate language, Shankman and Allen walk the reader through the relevant, potent lessons of emotionally intelligent leadership every active college student should understand. The combination of the authors' expertise with the voices of students across America creates the ideal framework of leadership upon which most any person could build."—*Jim Meehan, Case Western Reserve University*

"Kudos to Shankman and Allen for this unique tour through emotional intelligence, specifically geared toward students. I found this book refreshing and enlightening, and wish I had access to it in my formative years in undergraduate and graduate school."—*Darby Miller Steiger, national survey research consultant; contributing author,* The International Survey Handbook *(forthcoming)*

Emotionally Intelligent Leadership

A Guide for College Students

Marcy Levy Shankman
Scott J. Allen

Foreword by
Susan R. Komives

JOSSEY-BASS
A Wiley Imprint
www.josseybass.com

Published by Jossey-Bass
A Wiley Imprint
989 Market Street, San Francisco, CA 94103-1741—www.josseybass.com

Readers should be aware that Internet Web sites offered as citations and/or sources for further information may have changed or disappeared between the time this was written and when it is read.

Limit of Liability/Disclaimer of Warranty: While the publisher and author have used their best efforts in preparing this book, they make no representations or warranties with respect to the accuracy or completeness of the contents of this book and specifically disclaim any implied warranties of merchantability or fitness for a particular purpose. No warranty may be created or extended by sales representatives or written sales materials. The advice and strategies contained herein may not be suitable for your situation. You should consult with a professional where appropriate. Neither the publisher nor author shall be liable for any loss of profit or any other commercial damages, including but not limited to special, incidental, consequential, or other damages.

Jossey-Bass books and products are available through most bookstores. To contact Jossey-Bass directly call our Customer Care Department within the U.S. at 800-956-7739, outside the U.S. at 317-572-3986, or fax 317-572-4002.

Jossey-Bass also publishes its books in a variety of electronic formats. Some content that appears in print may not be available in electronic books.

ISBN: 978-0-4702-7713-3

Printed in the United States of America
FIRST EDITION
PB Printing   10 9 8

Contents

Part Three: Consciousness of Others — 73

Marcy dedicates
this book to her family, friends,
and colleagues who have always said that a book
was in her future—thank you for being right.

Scott would like to dedicate this book to a friend, brother,
and mentor—Robert L. Cottrell.

Foreword
It's All About Relationships

Followers

Participants

Collaborators

Constituents

Leaders

Facilitators

Change agents

How would you combine the concepts evoked by any of these words to explain leadership? In *Exploring Leadership: For College Students Who Want to Make a Difference* (Komives, Lucas, & McMahon, 2007), we viewed leadership as "a relational and ethical process of people together attempting to accomplish positive change" (p. 74). You may think of those people as leaders and followers; however, we assert that whether in positional or nonpositional roles, people in groups engage in the process of doing leadership together.

Critical to the leadership process is the capacity of each individual to engage in authentic relationships with others and to truly understand that *leadership is all about relationships*. Developing and maintaining healthy, effective relationships is all about emotional intelligence. Indeed, Allen and Cherrey (2000) observed, "relationships are the connective tissue of the organizations. . . . relationships built on trust and integrity, become the glue that holds us together" (p. 31). This book is designed to help you expand your personal capacity to effectively engage with others by focusing on your consciousness of yourself, your consciousness of others, and your consciousness of the context in which you engage in leadership together.

Expanding your relational capacity is the emotionally intelligent leadership that Marcy Shankman and Scott Allen present in this book. Consider your emotional quotient (EQ) like your intelligence quotient (IQ) and build your capacity to address intrapersonal awareness, interpersonal skills, adaptability, resilience, and general mood (Bar-On, 1997) in conjunction with how you would apply your IQ to expand your cognitive complexity. Caruso (2003) described the process we use in applying our emotional intelligence:

> We first accurately *identify* emotions. Second, we *use* these emotions to influence how we think and what we think about. Third, we attempt to *understand* the underlying causes of these emotions and determine how these emotions will change over time. Finally, we *manage* with emotions by integrating the wisdom of these feelings into our thinking, decision-making, and actions (p. 39).

You have a marvelous opportunity in college to learn and practice emotionally intelligent leadership. As Marcy and Scott note, you are in a remarkable "learning laboratory" where you engage with diverse others in both classroom contexts—such as in group projects and lab experiments, service learning, campus jobs—and a broad array of cocurricular contexts ranging from intramurals or ROTC to fraternities or sororities. Faculty, student affairs educators, counselors, graduate students, and upper-class peers provide a ready source of mentoring or a willing ear to listen to your reflections. These supports can become companions while you intentionally stretch yourself into this leadership journey. This is a journey into yourself, into empathic understanding of others, and into sharpening your awareness of context. This book crisply helps you explore important dimensions of learning to do that well.

Learning to relate effectively to others is a developmental process. As we noted in the preface to *Exploring Leadership* (Komives et al., 2007), you would not quit learning to play tennis when serve after serve went slamming into the net or landed outside the base line—you would practice. Similarly, when you are working with others in groups you can practice the dimensions of emotionally intelligent leadership outlined in this book to help you reach a deeper, authentic understanding of others. Most of us need constant practice and skill at relating effectively with diverse others as we work together to accomplish goals and tasks.

Our research on leadership identity development (Komives, Longerbeam, Owen, Mainella, & Osteen, 2006; Komives et al., 2007) showed it was very common for college students to think that the positional leader does leadership and that it is the role of followers to help the leader get the job done; indeed, many students would say that followers do followership. In this leader-centric philosophy of leadership, followers are dependent on the leader to set the direction and course of the group's work. As students' views of relationships develop, many come to an awareness that we are interdependent on each other in a group setting. The positional leader would value shared leadership and seek the active participation of group members. Group members realize they are doing leadership as active participants of the group. Each person in the group is doing leadership. One of our student participants in our research said, "I realized I can be a leader without a title." Leadership was viewed as a process among people working together in the group. This shift from hierarchical thinking to system thinking is complex, but it is developmental.

I challenge you to practice emotionally intelligent leadership with a goal to learn the interdependence of people working together in group settings. Whether you are in a positional leadership role or serve as an active member of the group, you are doing leadership! Your authentic, ethical relationships are centrally important to the group's community and to accomplishing your shared goals. Emotionally intelligent leadership, which you will learn about as you read this book, is central to your developmental process of learning to engage with others and do leadership together. Enjoy the journey—and keep practicing!

Susan R. Komives
Author of *Exploring Leadership: For College Students Who Want to Make a Difference* and coeditor of the *Handbook of Student Leadership Programs*

Acknowledgments

Writing this book has been a joyful ride from the beginning. We started the process over a cup of coffee, and ever since the cup has been overflowing—with good ideas, with challenging questions, and with incredible support. We gratefully acknowledge the contributions of the following individuals, and students from their institutions, for offering their views and ideas for us to incorporate into this book.

Jessica Allen, City Club of Cleveland

Aaron Asmundson, University of Minnesota

Colleen Barker-Williamson, Case Western Reserve University

Stephen Becker, Becker Consulting

Claudia Beeny, Bellarmine University

Cathy Clark, Appalachian State University

L. Martin Cobb, Beta Theta Pi Fraternity

Les Cook, Michigan Technological Institute

Steve Dealph, Miami University (Ohio)

Tiffany Hansbrough, Baldwin-Wallace College

Cori Holbert, Depaul University

Bill Jonas, The Catholic University of America

Marilyn Kempnich, University of Iowa

Charley Krebs, University of Wisconsin-Sheboygan

Arthur Leary, Case Western Reserve University (retired)
Jim Meehan, Case Western Reserve University
Marc Mores, Phi Delta Theta Fraternity
Laura Osteen, Florida State University
Mary Peterson, Sigma Lambda Gamma Sorority
David Pittman, Florida State University
Tracy Purinton, Massachusetts Institute of Technology
Tracy Stuck, The Ohio State University

About the Authors

Marcy Levy Shankman, Ph.D., has spent the last fifteen years facilitating leadership and organizational development experiences. After spending a number of years working directly with college students on campus, Marcy caught the entrepreneurial spirit and opened her own consulting practice, MLS Consulting, LLC, to expand her work to the nonprofit sector. Her focus is on enhancing the potential of individuals and organizations through custom-designed learning opportunities and organizational interventions. Her work is mainly with nonprofit organizations and educational institutions. Marcy has written two emotional intelligence assessments: the *EI Profile* and the *EI Full Spectrum*. In addition to her consulting work, Marcy teaches as a Presidential Fellow at Case Western Reserve University and as an instructor at Baldwin-Wallace College. Marcy lives in Shaker Heights, Ohio, with her husband, Brett, and two children—Rebecca and Joshua.

Scott J. Allen, Ph.D., started his career in the nonprofit sector, developing award-winning programs designed especially for the needs of emerging leaders. In 2005, Scott formed the Center for Leader Development (www.centerforleaderdevelopment.com), an organization created to provide resources, tools, and services to businesses, organizations, and schools seeking to build leadership capacity in their employees, members, or students. Scott is a visiting assistant professor at John Carroll University where he teaches strategic management, organizational behavior, business communication, management development, and human resources. He is published in the *Encyclopedia of Leadership* and coauthored *A Charge Nurse's Guide: Navigating the Path of Leadership*, a leadership book for health care professionals. In addition, he coauthored *The Little Book of Leadership: 50 Tips to Accelerate Leader Potential in Others* (Moonlight Publishing) with Mitch Kusy, Ph.D. Scott is an associate with the Larry Morrow Group and is involved with the Institute for Creative Leadership, LeaderShape, the International Leadership Association, Organization Development Institute, and the International Coach Federation. He resides in Cleveland, Ohio, with his wife, Jessica.

To contact the authors:

Marcy Levy Shankman
shankman@mlsconsulting.net
216.513.5673

Scott Allen
scott@cldmail.com
216.224.7072

Emotionally Intelligent Leadership

1

INTRODUCTION

All day I think about it, then at night I say it.
Where did I come from, and what am I supposed to
be doing?
I have no idea.
My soul is from elsewhere, I'm sure of that,
And I intend to end up there.
—*Rumi, thirteenth-century poet*

A search for the word *leadership* on Amazon.com returns more than 178,000 results. Amazingly, a similar search on Google yields 269 million hits! Consider that you can read over two thousand published definitions of leadership. Yet although the topic of leadership is far-reaching, surprisingly few books focus on leadership as it applies to college students.

Part of our motivation for writing this book is that we believe college students have a terrific "learning lab" at their disposal. The campus environment provides a rich and plentiful array of opportunities for students to practice leadership skills for four (or maybe five) years. Campus-based organizations, residence halls, teams, and related opportunities provide students with many different ways to get involved. Students can experiment with different approaches to leadership—honing the philosophy and style that best suits them.

This book will help you begin or enhance the development of your leadership potential. This book will also help you think more critically about the topic of leadership. Although you may know it when you are in the presence of a great leader, you may not know why you feel that way. You may also feel someone is not effective at leadership, but you may not know why. We hope you are on the path toward developing your leadership potential and becoming . . .

- The man or woman people look to in times of need
- The person who can be depended on to provide direction and guidance to others
- The person who wants to make a difference in the lives of others
- The one who is known for personal insights and strong convictions for the causes in which you believe
- The person who is known for an inclusive approach and the ability to work through differences

This book is about more than just being the leader. This book will also help you become a better *follower*—a role or position often left out of discussions on leadership.

So why read this book? What's in it for you? We hope you'll find a lot; however, it really depends on what you want to do with your time on campus and where you want to be in the future.

To some people, being in a leadership role sounds wonderful. Others may not aspire to a formal role. Whether you see yourself as a leader or not, chances are you'll have at least one opportunity in the future to demonstrate leadership. We believe that emotionally intelligent leadership (EIL) is an important topic for anyone who wants to demonstrate effective leadership. EIL provides a new lens through which to view the unique contributions that emotional intelligence adds to understanding and demonstrating leadership.

If you hope to lead others, this book will help you think about the role of leader in a new way. If you're interested in being a good team member, a good employee, or even a good friend, EIL will provide you with some of the tools needed to be successful in a formal (appointed) or informal (voluntary) leadership role.

If you are comfortable with the role of follower or with being involved informally, this book will help you clarify the skills and abilities that are important for effective leadership and follower-ship. EIL will help you increase your understanding of the type of leader you want to become or be aligned with. It will help you think about the type of organizations, groups, or offices you might want to join or work in one day. Finally, increasing your understanding of the various capacities of EIL will help you become more aware of who you are, what you want to do, and who you care about.

Consider this book as a gift—be willing to take from it what you can. Clarity on the various topics addressed throughout the book will, we hope, save you heartaches and headaches in the future. If you can learn more about yourself, how to work more productively with others, how to improve your relationships with others, and how to be more effective in a leadership role, you will be successful. Regardless of how you define effective leadership or what role you wish to play in it, it is incredibly important in today's world.

Foundational Thoughts

The premise of this book is that we all can develop our leadership abilities. Recent research conducted on twins corroborates this philosophy (Arvey, Rotundo, Johnson, & McGue, 2003). Arvey found that as much as 70 percent of leadership is learned. This is good news for all of us!

Another basic premise of this book is that the framework outlined is simply that. This framework can in no way cover the leadership capacities needed for *every* situation. For us to claim such a notion would be ludicrous. It would be similar to saying you need to know only twenty-two things to be a great basketball player or singer. We believe, however, that we have combined the work of some great student leaders and leadership theorists to present a new model for learning more about leadership and your own leadership potential.

Foundations of the EIL Model

The model of emotionally intelligent leadership has been developed in three ways. First, we (Marcy and Scott) bring our combined knowledge on the topic of leadership and leadership development. We each have spent many years working with college students from various campuses on the subject of leadership. In addition, EIL is the composite thinking of transformational leadership (Bass, 1985; Burns, 1978), situational leadership (Blanchard, 1991), contingency theory (Fiedler, 1972), leader-member exchange and emotional intelligence (Bar-On, 1997; Goleman, 1998; Goleman, Boyatzis, & McKee, 2002; Salovey, & Mayer, 1990; Segal, 1997; Weisinger, 1998), authentic leadership development (Avolio & Luthans, 2006), positive psychology, organizational culture, and organizational behavior. We have also incorporated the work of a number of scholars and organizations, such as John Gardner (1990), Howard Gardner (1999), Ronald Heifetz (1994), the Higher Education Research Institute (1996), and Joseph Rost (1993). Finally, we developed the model based on the thinking of your collegiate peers. We surveyed dozens of students from across North America, and their voices are present throughout the text.

Although we have used our knowledge, a large base of the literature, and your peers as a foundation, you can use this book as a guide to help you begin *your own* leadership journey. In addition, you can take comfort in the fact that, regardless of what various scholars or experts assert, your own experience and perspective have great value. We feel that all of us need to determine our own styles and approaches to leadership and followership. The key is the *intentionality* of our actions. In other words, just as with any other skill or ability, you have to *want* to develop it. Effective leadership takes commitment and awareness. Effective leadership takes a change in behavior. Effective leadership takes practice.

About Emotionally Intelligent Leadership

This model of emotionally intelligent leadership synthesizes two major bodies of research and theory: emotional intelligence and leadership. Throughout the book, the research and work of other scholars and practitioners is discussed as part of the EIL model.

In 1990, Peter Salovey and John Mayer published a scholarly paper in which they coined the term *emotional intelligence*. They defined EI as "the ability to monitor one's own and others' feelings and emotions to use the information to guide one's thinking and actions" (p. 189). In 1995, the term was made popular by Daniel Goleman in his book *Emotional Intelligence*. In his follow-up book, Goleman (1998) defined emotional intelligence as "the capacity for recognizing our own feelings and those of others, for motivating ourselves, and for managing emotions well in ourselves and in our relationships" (p. 317).

Foremost in this model of emotionally intelligent leadership, the leader must be conscious of three fundamental facets that contribute to the leadership dynamic: consciousness of context, self, and others. Figure 1.1 provides a visual of these three arenas.

Figure 1.1 Three Core Facets

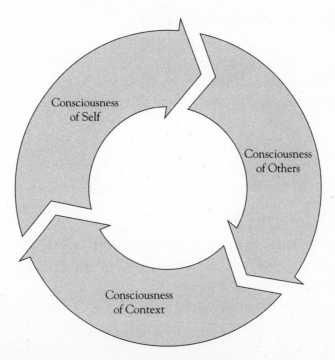

Consciousness of Self

Consciousness of Others

Consciousness of Context

Here is an example to clarify what is meant by consciousness of self, others, and context. Let's examine President John F. Kennedy as an exemplar of this model. President Kennedy (self) was elected at a time (context) when his personal leadership attributes and his message aligned with that being sought by the people of the United States (others). Would President Kennedy be elected today? No one knows. Based on our reading of theory and research on leadership, one thing is certain—were he to seek election today, Kennedy would need to align his message with issues that mesh with our current reality and context.

Effective leaders in any organization or sector of society ensure that their message resonates with the interests and desires of others (Goleman, Boyatzis, & McKee, 2002). Effective or ineffective leadership is therefore a relationship between these three facets: consciousness of context, consciousness of self, and consciousness of others. Leaders' ability to monitor all three intentionally will aid in their ability to lead effectively. After all, leaders must be aware of their capacities, the needs of those who follow them, and the environmental factors that come into play as well.

EIL consists of twenty-one capacities to which a leader should pay attention. In the *American Heritage Dictionary*, *capacity* is defined as "ability to perform or produce; capability." We chose this word because, as noted, everyone has the capacity to develop the ability to lead others effectively. The question comes down to choice—do we want to?

Emotionally Intelligent Leadership

Consciousness of Context

The environment in which leaders and followers work

Environmental awareness: Thinking intentionally about the environment of a leadership situation

Group savvy: Interpreting the situation and/or networks of an organization

Consciousness of Self

Being aware of yourself in terms of your abilities and emotions

Emotional self-perception: Identifying your emotions and reactions and their impact on you

Honest self-understanding: Being aware of your own strengths and limitations

Healthy self-esteem: Having a balanced sense of self

Emotional self-control: Consciously moderating your emotions and reactions

Authenticity: Being transparent and trustworthy

Flexibility: Being open and adaptive to changing situations

Achievement: Being driven to improve according to personal standards

Optimism: Being positive

Initiative: Wanting and seeking opportunities

Consciousness of Others

Being aware of your relationship with others and the role they play in the leadership equation

Empathy: Understanding others from their perspective

Citizenship: Recognizing and fulfilling your responsibility for others or the group

Inspiration: Motivating and moving others toward a shared vision

Influence: Demonstrating skills of persuasion

Coaching: Helping others enhance their skills and abilities

Change agent: Seeking out and working with others toward new directions

Conflict management: Identifying and resolving problems with others

Developing relationships: Creating connections between, among, and with people

Teamwork: Working effectively with others in a group

Capitalizing on difference: Building on assets that come from differences with others

If you are interested in developing your EIL, then you need a healthy balance of these capacities. There is no fixed formula for which capacities you must demonstrate; that would minimize the complexities and realities of leadership and of us as human beings.

We also believe that it is not effective or advisable to demonstrate any one of these capacities to excess. For instance, leaders can take teamwork to an extreme and become bogged down when trying to progress and move forward. On the other hand, leaders may completely negate the importance of teamwork and alienate themselves from the group. In addition, leaders with low capacity for empathy may have a difficult time convincing others to believe that they have others' best interests at heart.

The bottom line is that each capacity requires balance. The trick is that the right level of being in balance is dynamic—it's constantly shifting. In other words, an appropriate capacity for *developing relationships* in one context may be inadequate in others, based on the leader, the followers, and the context. The best leaders realize this, and they intentionally adjust their approaches or levels based on the needs of others and the context.

Leadership development is a long-term endeavor—a journey that all of us must consistently work on if we want to develop and grow. And as with any knowledge, skill, or ability, you need to reflect on your successes and failures, observe others whom you admire and respect, and engage in trusting relationships with people who will provide you with open and honest feedback. Finally, and perhaps most important, to demonstrate emotionally intelligent leadership you must transfer this knowledge into action.

What Lies Ahead: How to Use This Book

This book is intended to be a fast read. The chapters are short and contain our thoughts, the thoughts of experts, and student voices. The book is interactive. At the end of each chapter, specific questions are offered to deepen your thinking. We hope that as you read this book you will reflect on your life and how these concepts and capacities apply.

We suggest talking with a close friend or mentor about the topics and even the questions. If you have these conversations, we believe you will receive feedback that will help you identify opportunities for growth and existing areas of strength. If you are truly adventurous, talk with a couple of people—not just one. After all, your mom or dad knows you in a different way than your volleyball coach does. Each has valuable information to contribute toward your development and growth.

We are excited to join you on your leadership journey. Let's begin.

Part One

CONSCIOUSNESS OF CONTEXT

The Environment in Which Leaders and Followers Work

Environmental Awareness

Group Savvy

Leadership is a relationship between the leader (self), the followers (others), and the context. What does this mean? To every situation the leader brings certain knowledge, skills, and abilities. Some leaders may have an incredible amount of technical knowledge; others have a unique ability to motivate others through public speaking and motivation. The leader (self), however, is only one part of the equation.

Followers are the second part of the leadership equation, and they are often overlooked. After all, without followers, a leader has no one to lead! In actuality, followers often determine leadership success or failure. If a leader captures followers' hearts and minds, much can be accomplished. If not, very little will be accomplished.

> Environment can either make or break leadership ability.
> —*Female senior at University of Iowa, involved in an honor society, job/internship, and a religious organization*

Context is the third piece of the leadership dynamic. The context is the environment in which the leader and followers work (Fiedler, 1996); it is generally a combination of setting and situation. Setting refers to the structure of the organization; for example, a for-profit organization in corporate America, a college sports team, or any organization or group (formal or informal) in which the leader-follower relationship exists. The situation includes the many different forces of a particular time and place, including, but not limited to, individual personalities, organizational politics, and tensions or challenges within the setting. Situations are dynamic. The context may be filled with people who value being involved or it may not. Each new context requires a different set of knowledge, skills, and abilities on the part of leaders and followers. An example appears in the following section.

Context at Work

Think about a sports team. You have a coach (the leader), a group of players (the followers), and the context (the league rules, the other teams, the location, the season, and so on). The coach may use a certain style one year and experience great success given the players and the context. As team members and competing teams change, however, the coach will likely need to change her motivational style, the workouts, and her approach to the game to remain successful. If the coach is unable to understand and adapt to the needs of her players (followers) and the overall environment (the context), she may find herself in trouble.

Many of us, when we find ourselves in positions of leadership, are not consciously aware of the followers and the context. We may falsely assume that what has worked well in the past will work just as well in the future. If, or when, this does not work, we may externalize (blame others or outside factors). Consciousness of context reminds us to use our abilities to perceive and look inward as well as outward at what *we* could have done differently given the new or changing environment.

Here is another example. Imagine a teacher who has seen great success in teaching junior social studies at a strict Catholic school in a middle-class suburb. The students are not culturally diverse and are generally well-behaved. The teacher connects well with them and appreciates their structured environment. It seems that this teacher is successful in this context. Apparently his knowledge, skills, and abilities mesh well with the Catholic school environment (context) and the students (followers).

Now imagine this same teacher in a public school located in the Bronx. In addition, he is teaching middle school rather than high school students. See where we are going with this? He is still a teacher and still brings inherent knowledge, skills, and abilities to the table, but the change in context and followers will likely require him to use a number of new skills and behaviors. After all, the culture is different, the students are different, the socio-economic status is different—there are too many variables to mention.

The teacher's success will be determined (in part) by his ability to adjust to this new context. If he is not aware of this and is not intentionally approaching this situation with these concepts at the forefront of his mind, he will likely be swallowed up by change.

These examples illustrate consciousness of context. Think of a time when you experienced great success as a leader. Now think of a time when you failed. In all likelihood you were the same person, but perhaps everything else around you was different. Being aware of the context is vitally important to emotionally intelligent leadership.

Conclusion

The context of a situation provides many challenges and opportunities, even to the most seasoned leaders. What contextual factors existed in Germany that allowed Hitler to rise to power? Would Martin Luther King, Jr. have risen to the pinnacle of leadership in 1995? Would Bill Gates's idea of personal computers have been relevant in 2005? Your success as a leader often depends on your ability to inspire and meet the needs of followers and adjust to new and varied contexts.

2

ENVIRONMENTAL AWARENESS

Thinking Intentionally About the Environment of a Leadership Situation

Now that we have determined the important role of context in the leadership equation, let's take a closer look at how emotionally intelligent leaders manage their environment to enable (or demonstrate) leadership. This is the hard part: *intentionally* thinking about the environment in any leadership situation. Harvard faculty Ronald Heifetz and Marty Linsky (2002) call this "getting on the balcony" (p. 8).

> The environment acts as a catalyst or deterrent for everything you do.
> —*Male senior at Case Western Reserve University, involved in an honor society and athletics*

This means an individual has the ability to observe, in real time, the group dynamics and factors present in the environment. The leader can observe what is happening *from above*, like the proverbial fly on the wall.

Environmental Awareness in Action

To get a sense of how to recognize the influence of the environment on leadership, try an experiment. The next time you attend a meeting of an organization in which you are involved, pay close attention to what is going on around you. Think about the meeting and the organization as a whole. As you watch the meeting or activity, observe the following environmental factors:

- Who is the leader of the meeting?

- What have previous leaders been like? How have they been viewed by members or participants? Why are they viewed this way?

- What does your organization value? What values are implicitly known? Explicitly known? How do these values play into the success or failure of a leader?

- Who are the followers in the meeting?

  - What do they value?

  - What do they get from being a member of the organization?

  - Is there apathy among followers? If so, how do you know?

  - Are there many members or participants who readily point out problems but do little to help solve them? How does this affect the organization?

- How would you describe the context or environment?

  - Is the organization doing a good job of doing what it is intended to do? Are its activities and mission (reason for existence) consistent with each other?

  - Are members and leaders happy?

  - Is there pride in the organization? Is it doing "well" in the eyes of its members and constituents?

  - Is the campus community supportive of the organization? Is the organization seen as a benefit or detriment to the community?

As you reflect on these questions (and others), try to stay separate from the conversation. Simply observe. This is what it is like to "get on the balcony." Returning to a sports analogy, it's like the great basketball players who can both play and have an acute and real-time awareness of the overall game. They know where everyone is, how they will react, and what needs to be accomplished every step of the way in order to succeed.

Conclusion

Developing environmental awareness can be difficult. It is a skill that must be practiced intentionally. Why? For many, it is often human nature to jump in and react to stimuli rather than observe. Learning how and what to observe comes with experience. Want to see this in action? Try watching it play out at your next meeting. Leaders who are aware of their environments use that knowledge to determine a course of action.

Student Voice

"I believe environment has a great effect. If in a hostile or edgy environment, I might be hesitant and cautious when making suggestions or disagreeing with another's suggestion. In a more relaxed and friendly environment where members blend well in communication, I would feel more at ease in sharing openly my honest opinions."—*Female sophomore at Michigan Technological University, involved in the residence hall association*

———————

"The environment has everything to do with one's ability to lead. Everyone has a leadership style which comes naturally. Each style has positives and negatives for the environment. If the environment requires a leadership style not mastered by the leader, it becomes difficult to impact what goes on."—*Male senior at University of Cincinnati, involved in a fraternity, an honor society, and a professional society*

———————

"After this past summer, environment has a new meaning to me. If an environment has an established culture, it is harder to get adjusted and bring the people along with you. In an office, the environment describes the mood, almost to what I want to call the "integrity" of the company. If it's a positive environment, that's great, but when it lacks support and communication, there is room for error and even failure."—*Female fifth-year senior at Florida State University, involved in a sorority and a job/internship*

Reflection Questions

- When serving in a leadership role, are you able to "get on the balcony" or do you always find yourself jumping into the conversation? What are the implications of this?
- What is the potential drawback of "getting on the balcony" too often?
- In what environments do you have the greatest success as a leader? Which environments are the most challenging? Why?

3

GROUP SAVVY

Interpreting the Situation and/or Networks of an Organization

Imagine that you're new to a group. Maybe you have an internship or a part-time job in an office. Or maybe you're a new member in an organization or club. Perhaps you have a new group of friends. When you're new, one of the big questions is, how do you become a part of that group? How do you figure out where you fit?

If you're working, you may go through a staff orientation. Colleges and universities run orientation programs so that new students can learn about life on campus. But is this enough? If you've joined a club or organization, do you get anything more than an introduction to the people and an explanation of "how we do things here"? What if no one tells you any of this? If or when an introduction or orientation occurs, you generally get the official or accepted policies, procedures, rules, and regulations. We all know, however, that there's a lot about being in a group that isn't written down, explained, or even necessarily clearly defined.

> [Group savvy is] not something someone can teach you. I may be able to guide you, but politics is something you must learn on your own by experience.
> —*Female junior at The Ohio State University, involved in a sorority, athletics, a job/internship, and volunteer work*

Group savvy describes the skill set that helps you in all of these scenarios. This EIL capacity entails reading between the lines, identifying the "power players" in a group, and knowing how to get along without being told what to do and how to do it every step of the way. Group savvy helps you learn organizational politics and values. You can identify who is important in a group and how to develop relationships so you fit in. You can figure out what is happening and how to help make things happen.

Peeling Away the Layers

Imagine an onion. On the outside are the brown protective layers of skin. As you peel away the layers, the skin changes texture from papery and fragile to something stronger. At the middle of the onion, you find the most pungent and powerful part. Imagine an onion as a metaphor for a relationship or a group.

There are elements of a group that are known and obvious— who is in charge by title or position, the written rules of the group, and so on. These are the outer layers of the onion—easy to get at and clearly known to everyone (Hunt, 1991). But as you peel away the easy layers, you get to the tougher, stronger layers. Who is actually in charge? What matters most to the group? Who forms the in-group, and who are the outsiders? These questions help you understand the group or organization in a deeper way. When you ask these questions and discover the answers, you are using your group savvy skills.

Diagnosis

Diagnosing an organization or group culture is at the core of group savvy. Understanding what is going on in a group might mean learning the difference between what you are officially told and what you perceive really happens. Consider learning about an organization or group culture in order to improve your group savvy. According to Driskill and Brenton (2005), the following elements make up a group's culture:

- *Symbolic elements:* This category refers to aspects of culture that represent something of value; for example, logos, formal speeches, web pages, organizational stories, even slang used by group members.

- *Role elements:* This category refers to the two main roles that help you understand a group's culture—the heroes (people within the organization whom everyone admires) and the villains (the bad guys and girls, rebels).
- *Interactive elements:* This category includes the rituals, group norms, accepted behaviors, and communication styles demonstrated by group members and by the group itself.
- *Context elements:* This category reflects the important roles that place and time play in an organization. An organization's culture is affected by its history, location, and space (both physical space and the context in which the organization exists in relation to its external environment).

Learning to recognize and understand these elements enhances your ability to figure out what's going on in a group—your group savvy. Becoming familiar with these different elements of an organization's culture also enables you to become a more active participant in that group.

The Power of Asking Questions

Group savvy represents a set of skills developed through experience. You learn how to navigate a group by being in an organization. You develop your capacity to perceive and read the social and power networks by becoming part of the networks themselves. Try this: think about the different elements mentioned earlier. Focus on an organization or group that you know well—it could be a club or organization, a workplace, or even a group of friends. Think about how these elements affect leadership. As you reflect on the relationship between these elements and leadership, you'll begin to see your group or organization in a whole new light. Here are a few questions to get you started:

- Who is the leader of the meeting?
- In your opinion, what are the leader's strengths and weaknesses?

- What would make the leader more successful or influential?
- What knowledge, skills, or abilities elevated the leader to this role? Knowledge? Friendliness? Did this person simply *do* a lot?
- Who are the followers in the meeting?
- Are the followers subservient or are they independent-minded?
- Does anyone seem to have a personal agenda? Is this person supportive of the leader? Why or why not?
- Who speaks a lot? Who speaks but is not heard or given power by the group or the leader?

Conclusion

Organizations are complex and dynamic. What works in one group or for one organization may fail miserably in another. The same holds true for leadership—a leader in one organization may not be successful in another. There are many examples of corporate, educational, and political leaders who are successful in one position and fall short of expectations when they change companies, institutions, or offices. Group savvy helps leaders improve their navigation of the challenges and complexities of different organizations.

Student Voice

"When I'm first joining an organization, I always limit my active participation. Instead, I spend a lot of time watching the body language of long-time members. I notice (1) their manner of interaction with each other and (2) their reaction to other newcomers in the group. From these interactions, I infer social norms. Following the internal rules of the organization lets me get what I want out of the organization. For example, I have to act brashly in my college dormitory if I want anyone to notice me, but that sort of attitude would have gotten me fired from my summer internship."—*Female senior at MIT, involved in volunteer work, internship/job, and a religious organization*

"Clearly, the easiest way to learn the unwritten rules or internal workings of an organization is to be fully engulfed in the organization. By carefully listening and evaluating an organization, an individual can quickly (this being a very relative term) discover the internal workings and organizational culture that exists within an organization."—*Male senior at University of Nebraska–Lincoln, involved in a fraternity and an honor society*

"To be honest, the best way is to enter a position and learn through mistakes. This can be best done if you provide an acclimation period wherein outgoing executive and incoming executive work as a pair for a substantial period of time to truly understand the internal workings of an organization."—*Male junior at Miami University (Ohio), involved in a fraternity, an honor society, and the residence hall association*

"I've learned these unwritten rules mostly by observation and listening. If I see how things operate and try to follow the examples of others, I find that I catch on quickly. I always ask questions if I don't think I'm doing something right."—*Female senior at University of Iowa, involved in orientation and an honor society*

Reflection Questions

- How does group savvy enhance your leadership potential?
- How does group savvy relate to environmental awareness or consciousness of context?
- How can you develop your awareness of the listed indicators of organizational culture?

Part Two

CONSCIOUSNESS OF SELF

Being Aware of Yourself in Terms of Your Abilities and Emotions

Emotional Self-Perception

Honest Self-Understanding

Healthy Self-Esteem

Emotional Self-Control

Authenticity

Flexibility

Achievement

Optimism

Initiative

Who are you? What are your goals, dreams, or aspirations? What are your hot buttons? What motivates you? What frustrates you? In what kind of environment do you perform best? Your answers to these and other questions are some of the secrets to your success as a leader.

Consciousness of self is all about you. Knowing who you are, what you stand for, and how your answers and actions can affect

> To identify your own emotions, reactions, and possibly their impact, you have to first know yourself.
> —*Male junior in the College of Engineering, involved in athletics, volunteering, and a religious organization*

others are all components of consciousness of self (Higher Education Research Institute, 1996). The good news is this: you have your entire life to work on consciousness of self. Just like any other EIL capacity, however, this takes effort. If you are not working to better understand your motives, values, and inner workings, who will? It is not important that this introspection results in concrete answers—it is the *process* of introspection that is important. For instance, think back to the last time you had fun. What was it that made you feel this way? Who were you with? What were you doing? Did you feel motivated? Having an awareness of these and other factors can help you create more happiness.

Here is a final concept before we begin this part. Simple awareness is not enough. Your words and actions must be closely aligned. As we go through life, most of us will have the experience of working for a boss or an organization that claims to value the customer or employee, yet their actions are the complete opposite. Leaders whose words match their actions truly exhibit consciousness of self. They are aware of how the two must align to yield long-term success. Doing so fosters trust in others, which is a core ingredient for those hoping to lead.

4

EMOTIONAL SELF-PERCEPTION

Identifying Your Emotions and
Reactions and Their Impact

Leadership development is a lifelong endeavor. Leaders emerge and evolve over time. Research shows that one of the primary foundations of leadership and leadership development is self-awareness or emotional self-perception (Avolio & Luthans, 2006; Conger, 1992; Goleman, Boyatzis, and McKee, 2002). We define emotional self-perception as the capacity to identify your emotions and reactions, and understanding their effects on you. This is a difficult capacity to master. In essence, it requires that you be in tune with your emotions—all the time.

Know Yourself

For instance, think about your brother, sister, or another family member who has the ability to get under your skin. This person's comments, actions, and behaviors take your level of frustration from 0 to 10 in mere seconds. We assume (if you are like us) you often go directly to 10 *and then* react. How you react may be through anger, yelling, crying, shutting down, or any number of other immediate responses. Your reactions may be either emotional (feeling angry), behavioral (yelling), or both.

Emotional self-perception means that you have the ability to be acutely aware of how you are feeling in real time (similar to the concept of "getting on the balcony" discussed previously). In other words, you are aware that frustration levels are rising. Having emotional self-perception also means you know that you have

We're college students and still learning how to react in professional or appropriate ways, and sometimes our younger sides get the better of us. You realize five minutes after you blew up at Sally or Joe that it was inappropriate, but that does let you practice apologizing, which is an important skill for a leader to have.

—*Female senior at Florida State University, involved in student government, volunteering, and a religious organization*

a *choice* as to how you respond. Generally, both healthy and unhealthy responses are available. For many, this is rarely a choice—we react immediately or instinctively to the stimulus.

To see this concept demonstrated, watch an episode of MTV's *The Real World*. It seems as if housemates often have little knowledge of their feelings, how those feelings affect their behavior, and how those behaviors affect those around them. It is interesting to watch the show through the lens of self-awareness. You can't completely fault the reality show stars—they have merely allowed their process of growth and development to be filmed.

Emotional Self-Perception and Leadership

Demonstrating emotional self-perception means that you can move beyond instinctive responses to a higher level of consciousness and action. Aligning this capacity with leadership, you can see the importance of this skill. For example:

Jim M. is a leader of the University Programming Board (UPB), and the officers are preparing for a large event on campus. Jim has consistently had trouble getting others to follow through with tasks and assignments. As a result, Jim's frustration level has consistently increased, and rather than confronting others or asking why they are not completing their jobs, he completes a great majority of tasks on his own—increasing his frustration. When he does see officers doing their work, his comments are less than positive, increasing their frustration levels as well. They begin talking behind his back and feel left out. By the time the event is over, the gap between Jim and the officers is wide—Jim blames the officers and they blame him for his inability to lead. The issue is never confronted.

What brought Jim to this point? In part, it may be that Jim does not realize that his current approach is not working—he is lacking emotional self-perception. For whatever reason, this message or style is not connecting with the others. This can be frustrating for a leader, and often we witness the leader's natural response, which may be to blame others or *externalize* the failure—"We would be fine if *they* would just do what they said they would!"

When this happens, frustration sets in. The leader may make comments that increase the gap between leader and followers—increasing annoyance on all levels. In the preceding scenario, if Jim had been acutely aware of his feelings and how they could affect his ability to lead, he could have confronted the issue in a positive manner at the beginning and, perhaps, avoided the whole problem.

Jim could have learned a lot through open dialogue with his officers—the source of apathy, what would motivate them, and so forth. Of course, it is not totally Jim's fault, but if his goal was to lead the organization through a successful event, letting his aggravation get the best of him did not help the situation. After all, who wants to be led by an individual who is inconsistent, lacking in self-awareness, and unaware of how his emotions and actions affect those around him?

> I think as a leader it is OK to identify your emotions and reactions. It is necessary to gain the trust of the people. Leaders must be able to admit their mistakes, faults, victories, etc. or their work will be meaningless.
> —*Female freshman at Baldwin-Wallace College, involved in an honor society, psychology club, and wind ensemble*

No one wants to be that person. You need to work consistently to remain connected with your feelings. You have to be aware of your hot buttons. If you stay in tune with those people and situations that can take you from 0 to 10 in moments, you can prepare before entering these situations. If or when you "fall off the wagon" and react in a manner we (or others) deem inappropriate, you need to examine the triggers. You can work to be acutely aware of how your emotions, feelings, and behaviors affect others. Doing so will provide you with invaluable feedback. Consider the words of the Chinese philosopher Confucius: "A journey of a thousand miles begins with a single step."

What will be your first step?

Student Voice

"Carefully watch and monitor the reactions of others when you display emotion. Try to gauge the strength and severity (either positive or negative reaction) to change your levels of emotional expression to best fit the group. If you feel the impact of your expression was regarded with more importance or impact than it should have been, you should not be afraid to explain or reiterate the true intention or meaning."—*Female senior at University of Iowa, involved in a job/internship and as a peer writing tutor*

"I usually edit my actions and responses in my mind before actually doing them. But sometimes my emotion gets the best of me, and I just blurt things out."—*Anonymous*

"I think that this is something that very few people actually can accomplish. I think that this is only something that can be developed through intense and deep personal experiences that may cause individuals to evaluate their actions. I do not feel that many people do this on a daily basis."—*Female senior at Michigan Technological University, involved in a professional organization, job/internship, and an honor society*

"You should know what events (significant and some minor) have occurred in your life so the real answer is reflection. Why do I do things the way I do? Why does one thing upset me but another doesn't? Why did I do it that way and not this way? What are my motivations? Why do I feel this way? Do I have a reason to feel this way? Where am I going at this point in my life? How did that event (or person) at X time affect my life and make me who I am today? I think you get the point. If you truly know yourself, you can better identify emotions, reactions, and predict impacts. You are the one who knows yourself best. Make sure you question yourself at different times, and you will find out more about yourself."—*Male junior in the College of Engineering, involved in athletics, volunteer work, and a religious organization*

Reflection Questions

- What kind of people do you find challenging to work with? What happens to you when you are around these people? How do you work through this?

- Who energizes you as a leader? As a follower? What happens when you are around people whom you find energizing? How do you feel?

- What are your blind spots? What happens when you become frustrated with a situation? Do you check out? Take over? Become argumentative?

5

HONEST SELF-UNDERSTANDING

Being Aware of Your Own Strengths and Limitations

Imagine a mirror that reflects a picture of your abilities. In this reflection you see your strengths and limitations, your talents and skills. This mirror helps you develop a clear understanding of what you are capable of and what gives you energy. You see those things that are challenging to you and those things that exhaust you. This image shows you aspects of yourself that make you proud and confident. You also see facets of your identity that might challenge or hurt your sense of self.

Honest self-understanding means that you celebrate and honor your strengths and talents while acknowledging your limitations. Knowing who you are means accepting the good and bad about your personality, abilities, and ideas. When you possess honest self-understanding you are more likely to demonstrate effective leadership, develop robust relationships, and have healthy self-esteem.

Know Thyself

Throughout our lives, we have many opportunities to learn more about ourselves. These opportunities are occasions for enhancing our self-understanding; however, we often miss these moments. We're too busy. We're not thinking about how we can learn from our experiences. We don't think that reflecting on the past is as important as moving ahead.

> If a leader does not know his or her weaknesses, those weaknesses will negatively affect her constituents.
>
> —*Female junior at The Catholic University of America, involved in an honor society, athletics, religious organization, student government, and the residence hall association*

When you miss these opportunities for reflection, you deplete your own resources. By not reflecting on what's happened, you don't take the time to think through your actions, how your actions may have affected others, or how you might have acted in different ways. As we have discussed, for leaders to be effective they must know themselves. As author and founder of the American Leadership Forum Joe Jaworski (1998) says, "Before you can lead others, before you can help others, you have to discover yourself."

Seek Feedback

One of the best ways to boost your self-understanding is to ask for feedback from people you know and trust to tell you the truth. Although it may be difficult to ask, it is an incredibly powerful way to enhance your sense of self.

How do you do this? The first step is to ask for the feedback. You have to find the right time to do so—the middle of a meeting or when you pass someone on the sidewalk isn't the best time to have this conversation. Plan and think through *when* to ask. You should be sure that you both have time for a focused and meaningful conversation.

Consider, also, *who* will give you meaningful feedback:

- Will this person be able to comment on your skills and abilities?
- Do you respect this person's opinion? If not, then don't bother asking.

- In what ways will this person contribute to advancing your understanding of yourself?
- Who are the people who can share their thoughts about you based on different contexts or situations?

Next, think about *how* to ask for feedback. The following are sample questions that you may use.

- In what way do you think I've been successful in. . . ?
- How could I have done . . . better? (Fill in the blank with whatever behavior or action you want to know more about.)
- Based on what you've experienced when working with me, what do you think I do well? Where do you think I could improve?

Learn to Hear the Positive and the Negative

Perhaps the most challenging aspect of asking for feedback is hearing it. Most people, when asked whether they like getting feedback, say no. This is often true for positive as well as negative feedback. After all, for some, hearing a compliment is as hard as hearing a criticism.

The first step is to prepare. If you've asked the right people for feedback, then you know they have your best interests at heart. When you ask people to help, you need to keep in mind that is what they are trying to do. Learning how to be gracious about what is said is a huge challenge. One way to show appreciation, regardless of the feedback, is to offer sincere thanks. Remember, you *always* have a choice in what you accept to be true. You may agree immediately. You may reject it as being off base. Or you may contemplate what is said, sort through how accurate it might be, and then decide whether to accept it.

Consider feedback as a gift. Show appreciation for someone's efforts in sharing thoughts with you. Then think about the possibilities. Remember that just because people share thoughts with you doesn't mean they're true—it's their perception. Consider the feedback honestly. Feedback that is difficult to hear has a positive side to it, but sometimes you have to work to find or accept it. Honest self-understanding is up to you and what you choose to do. You can make the most of feedback by using it to enhance what you know about yourself.

Student Voice

"When the group senses that the leader does not believe in his or her own abilities, each group member might try to take on the leadership role, creating no true facilitator and slowing things down."—*Female senior at University of Iowa, involved in a job/internship and as a peer writing tutor*

"The confidence of leadership carries throughout a whole group when it is there to be seen."—*Male sophomore at Michigan Technological University, involved in a fraternity, university programming board, volunteer work, and a job/internship*

Reflection Questions

- What aspect(s) of yourself would you like to know more about? Who can help you learn more?
- What behaviors do you need to develop as a leader (or follower)? Which can you further capitalize on?
- What do you believe are your greatest strengths? Try to find someone who knows you well and see if they identify the same set of assets. If not, where are the gaps? What does it mean when you believe yourself to be strong in an area that someone else doesn't?
- What are your limitations? How do they affect you?

6

HEALTHY SELF-ESTEEM

Having a Balanced Sense of Self

Unlike many EIL capacities, healthy self-esteem is fairly abstract. Simple definitions of self-esteem include feeling good about yourself and having a sense of who you are. Healthy self-esteem means believing in your abilities, knowing yourself well enough to stand up for what you believe in, and being strong when you feel challenged. The "healthy" part means that you hold yourself in check—that you have some humility. This humility helps you have a balanced sense of self.

> Healthy self-esteem can be seen across a room . . . the person is not arrogant. She carefully considers her thoughts and is willing to change her opinions . . . Her self-worth is not tied to being correct all the time.
> —*Female senior at MIT, involved in an honor society, volunteer work, and a religious organization*

Self-esteem is related to self-confidence. Self-confidence means you feel comfortable with who you are. You have a sense of your own potential. You believe in yourself and your abilities. But if any of these feelings are too strong, the positive turns into a negative. Too much self-esteem or self-confidence leads to arrogance, and we know where too much arrogance leads. So be sensitive to the healthy part of this capacity, and you'll find yourself a stronger candidate for demonstrating emotionally intelligent leadership.

Love Yourself First

The other day Marcy's seven-year-old daughter said, "You know Mommy, it's really important to love yourself first." When asked why, she said, "Well, you know, if you don't love yourself first, then how can you love anyone else?"

Sometimes the wisdom of a child is overwhelming.

As many of us know, life often makes it hard for us to love ourselves. Societal pressures and expectations can make it hard to be happy with who you are. Maybe you're not smart, attractive, strong, brave, or_____enough (fill in the blank with any of a number of adjectives). Even those who love you have expectations about who or what you should be. You are bombarded with the challenge of becoming who you were meant to be.

Being versus Becoming

Robert L. Payton—philanthropist, author, former United States ambassador, former college president, and friend—once told a story of how he wanted to be a paratrooper in the U.S. Army. His experience during training taught him about the difference between *being* a paratrooper and *becoming* one. To become a paratrooper, he had to practice jumping out of airplanes. The experience of actually jumping taught him that the first challenge in *being* someone is the process of *becoming* that person. Sometimes, *becoming* that person is too difficult—it challenges our sense of who we are to such a degree that our self-esteem gets shaken or even shattered. What has your experience been with this concept? Can you think of an example? Maybe you wanted to be a business major, but didn't become one because you couldn't pass calculus. Or you want to be a doctor, but dislike biology.

Giving In versus Giving Up

The challenge of acquiring and sustaining healthy self-esteem is that, similar to leadership development, it is an ongoing, lifelong process. Unlike an innate talent, healthy self-esteem is both an attitude and an ability. You feel and demonstrate your self-esteem daily, if not hourly. From a difficult conversation with a friend or parent to a hard class, you constantly face challenges to having or demonstrating healthy self-esteem.

Because of constant pressures, you need to learn how to consider the potential costs of a challenge to develop or maintain a healthy sense of who you are. What if the challenge is so great that you'll feel lousy if you don't succeed? If you feel lousy, will it be for an hour, a day, or always? When do you accept or give in to a challenge in order to save your self-esteem? Giving in to a challenge might be a short-term loss for the long-term gain of maintaining your healthy self-esteem. Giving in is different from giving up: giving in is a conscious choice based on reflection and analysis, whereas giving up is quitting or taking the easy way out without considering what else might be possible.

Healthy Self-Esteem in Action

Imagine having an emotional bank account (Covey, 1989). Every time something goes well, a deposit is made into the account. When something happens that causes you pain, a withdrawal is made. Healthy self-esteem exists when your bank account is comfortably above the minimum balance. Clearly this level is different for each of us. That's one of the great challenges of understanding self-esteem.

Think of a time when you were a part of a group that made you feel great just by being together. When you are in the presence of others who make you feel good, you get a big deposit in the emotional bank account—and your self-esteem benefits. You are more likely to feel good about yourself and develop a sense of the possible—you believe that you can accomplish what you want, you are competent, and you appreciate your capabilities. When it is at a healthy level, the emotional bank account gives you a safety net as well as a foundation upon which to build. This state of mind sets up the action side of self-esteem—it provides energy, inner strength, and power (Avolio & Luthans, 2006).

In a leadership context, healthy self-esteem radiates, positively affecting those around you. This capacity is contagious. The feelings generated can support you in making a big decision about what you want to accomplish as an individual or as a member of a group. You may feel more motivated to work with others on a task that is challenging and important. You have the confidence to take risks.

Remember, though, that too much self-esteem can be detrimental. If self-esteem is not held in check, you can develop arrogance or an unwieldy ego. You can become dismissive of other people. Too much confidence can be overwhelming to others, even to the point of damaging relationships or making unwise decisions. That's why this EIL capacity is called healthy self-esteem. When you are balanced, you position yourself well to do your best and, as a result, you can help bring out the best in others.

Student Voice

"Healthy self-esteem is like a tree. At a young age, the tree takes time to build strong branches and trunk. As it grows, it matures and becomes more sure of itself and what it is going to be. A fully grown tree stands tall and strong and sure of itself, as healthy self-esteem should. The most important part is, even though the tree is large, tall and strong with broad leaves and thick branches, there is always room for growth."—*Male senior at The Catholic University of America, involved in a professional organization, an honor society, and student government*

"Healthy self-esteem includes a person accepting himself for who he is. A person with healthy self-esteem takes pride in who he is and does not need to shun others to make himself feel better."—*Female sophomore at University of Wisconsin–Sheboygan, involved in volunteer work and a job/internship*

"Healthy self-esteem is being able to distinguish the neuroses in your head from the reality that everyone else can see."—*Female senior at Florida State University, involved in an honor society, university programming board, professional organizations, and volunteer work*

Reflection Questions

- On a scale of 1 to 10, with 10 being the highest, how would you rate your level of self-esteem?
- When do you feel at your best? Think about the context, what you're doing, and who you're with.
- Think about someone you know who seems to have healthy self-esteem. How do you know? How do you feel when you're with this person?

7

EMOTIONAL SELF-CONTROL

Consciously Moderating Your Emotions and Reactions

"It is our emotions that release us from paralysis and motivate us to act," said Jeanne Segal (1997, p. 16), author of the book *Raising Your Emotional Intelligence*. Although feeling our emotions and being aware of them is part of this statement, so too is regulating them. None of us wants to be an emotional volcano—exploding with emotions with little to no warning. Self-control is about both awareness (being conscious of what we're feeling) and action (being able to manage our emotions and knowing when and how to show them). Two important aspects of emotional self-control are recognizing how stress affects us and being aware of our hot buttons.

Reactions and Stress

Consider the following scenario: You're with friends when you discover that a friend in whom you have confided has shared your important and private matter with others. You're hurt and angry.

Option One: Emotional Worst-Case Scenario. You explode! You berate your friend, swearing that you will never trust him again. You shout (or perhaps coldly declare) your anger in a hurtful manner. Realizing what you've said, you turn bright red with embarrassment and become speechless. Everyone around you is staring, but you're still seething.

Option Two: Emotionally Intelligent Scenario. You take a deep breath. You ask your friend for a private moment. In a serious and calm tone, you share honestly how you feel knowing that your confidence has been betrayed. You express that you are hurt and offended by his action. You also share that you are unsure of how this will affect your relationship in the long run. You ask your friend to please not say anything to anyone else about this situation. Then you both rejoin the group, and you move to give yourself space from this person.

Who Will You Be?

Often, the difference between Options One and Two comes down to what else is going on in your life. You have the choice to go either way—we all do. In life, stress is an ever-present reality. The stress may be physical, brought about by a lack of sleep, or emotional. You have too much to do, and you feel the pressure to succeed. Regardless of the source of the stress, the difference in how you manage a situation and how much control you have over your impulses comes down to your consciousness of self. Emotional self-control is about regulation. You manage your emotions; you do not need to suppress them.

> I asked an e-board member not to publicize an event until we had finished planning it, and he did anyway. I was so angry with him (and already very stressed) but, instead of yelling, I asked him why he did it and he actually had a pretty good reason. It turns out that he wanted to get our event out to the public before another organization took our idea.
>
> —*Anonymous*

How much tolerance do you have when something triggers an emotional reaction? If you're managing your stress, it's likely that you'll have a greater chance of choosing Option Two, or something like it. On the other hand, if you're under a lot of stress, your tolerance and consciousness of self will be lowered, as will your ability to control emotional outbursts.

Hot Buttons

In large measure, moderating your emotions is about knowing yourself well and knowing what triggers your reactions. A trigger is something that is said or done that immediately causes an instinctive reaction, such as butterflies in your stomach or fierce anger. This reaction is part of your biological make-up. You are programmed, as a living being, to have a flight or fight reaction. Triggers activate that part of your brain that is most primitive; therefore your ability to become aware of them requires higher-order thinking. This process is one of the neurobiological differences between human beings and the rest of the animal world.

What topics or issues cause your heart to race? Are there certain subjects that you will immediately fight for or take a stand on no matter who you're with? Knowing your hot buttons and anticipating when they might be pushed are important steps toward managing your emotions. If you can develop your consciousness to know these triggers, you can prevent instinctive reactions from becoming your only reactions. You may not be able to control the emotional impulse, but you can manage these impulses by regulating your thoughts, decisions, and behaviors. This anticipation, through emotional self-control, can prevent you from exploding with rage and instead allow you to explain rationally why you feel the way you do. This awareness can also help modulate your feelings according to the context.

> Leaders who are not stable or who cannot reasonably control their emotions place the entire group as well as the individual members in a state of flux that is most likely not healthy nor conducive to progress.
> —*Anonymous*

Conclusion

The capacity of emotional self-control encompasses both an attitude and an ability. Be aware of your triggers and emotional reactions. You can also learn how to control your impulses and demonstrate emotions conscientiously. Emotional self-control, and EIL for that matter, recognizes that emotions are an important part of your life. Like it or not, emotions affect your thoughts, decisions, and behaviors. Emotionally intelligent leaders learn how to use their emotions effectively.

Student Voice

"I was working under a person who would continuously use my ideas as well as those of another coworker as his own. He would also pawn off mistakes that he had made on us. On many occasions, I wanted to give him a piece of my mind using as many profanities as possible, but we were being watched by others at all times, whether we knew it or not, and had to act accordingly. It was hard, because I am only human and I am young. I am still very much driven by my emotions, and I need to develop strategies to control them."—*Female senior at The Catholic University of America, involved in the residence hall association, a job/internship, and a religious organization*

"As a student leader dealing with disciplinary actions, I have frequently had to moderate my emotions, which would have had me extremely upset at a person for putting themselves and others in danger, and focus on how I could help the individual work through this problem and prevent it from happening again. Removing my emotion helped allow me to see beyond a solitary event and see how solving the underlying problem might improve that individual's life in the long term."—*Male senior at University of Nebraska–Lincoln, involved in a fraternity, honor society, professional organization, and volunteer work*

"I was running rather hot to begin with that day, and this girl was in my dorm room talking with my roommate, and she said something that just made me boil. I said two things and realized that it was going to get nasty if I didn't leave. So I took a breath and said goodbye and left with some friend. When I got outside, I was feeling better. Around others in general, I keep my emotions in check because I do not see it as useful to let emotion into many group decisions or projects. This can be difficult to master for students if they came from homes where emotion was frowned upon or where if they acted up they got what they wanted. There is also the stress a university can bring. The stress to succeed and also be social can be tough for some students to handle and, as a result, they do not control their emotions in a safe way."—*Male sophomore at Michigan Technological University, involved in a fraternity, university programming board, volunteer work, and a job/internship*

"I am a non-traditional student and am already in the work world as a writer. A few weeks ago, I had an assignment in one of my classes to write an op-ed paper. I received a "B" on it, and initially was almost insulted, since this is the work I do professionally (my professor did not know this). Then, after thinking about it, I thought I should not take it personally since the professor could be looking for something in the paper beyond what I do in my 'work writing.' I decided just to learn from the experience."—*Female freshman at University of Wisconsin–Sheboygan*

Reflection Questions

- What are your hot-button topics? How might you react in an emotionally intelligent way the next time this topic is raised?
- When you've seen someone lose control, how did others react? How was the setting affected?
- How does losing control of emotions affect a leader?

in alignment with what you value and believe.

8

AUTHENTICITY

Being Transparent and Trustworthy

You've probably heard the saying, "Be the same on the outside as you are on the inside"—in other words, be authentic. However, this can be difficult.

Authenticity is about many things—being true to who you are, being trustworthy, and being transparent so that your words match your actions and vice versa. This is no small order. Being authentic means, in part, that you keep your promises. That sounds simple, but it is not. You must know yourself well enough to know what you can honestly commit to. Often the hardest part about being authentic is in the action—do you follow through on what you commit to? Are you acting in alignment with what you value and believe?

Words alone do not constitute authenticity. Authenticity is based in action, and actions speak louder than words. Although you may believe you are authentic, others may see you differently. And their perception is reality. Images, as they say, are fragile.

No More Hidden Agendas

How many times have you heard about someone not fulfilling a promise? Or, even worse, what happens when the person does something opposite of what was promised? Both of these scenarios are frustrating and demonstrate behavior that is not authentic. Consider another example:

A small non-profit organization is going through an important growth phase. It is moving from a local, grassroots collaborative to a more professional, highly visible regional organization. The bylaws—the formal rules that govern the organization—need to be revised, so a small committee of volunteers forms to update the bylaws.

After the committee convenes, another person volunteers to join. Although it's late in the game, she promises to bring her experience with another organization that has just recently gone through this process. The chair of the committee enthusiastically welcomes this person to the committee. The work begins with all the members of the committee agreeing to the primary areas for revision and the desired result.

As bylaw revisions are suggested, the new member to the committee continually presents challenges to these ideas. She identifies a problem for each proposed revision: "It will cost too much money"; "This might insult the founding members of the group"; and "Oh, that won't work. Organizing the volunteers will just cause confusion."

On the surface, each one of these concerns makes sense. However, a problem emerges because these challenges are about something other than the new ideas. The lead staff person discovers that this person did not buy into the original agreement. The woman who joined the committee late simply wanted to be involved so she could prevent the bylaws from changing.

In the end, the committee spent three times as long as originally intended in order to satisfy this person. Although this volunteer said from the outset that she agreed with the purpose of the change, it turned out that she had an ulterior motive. Through thoughtful analysis of the issues, the leaders of this committee realized that this woman's motivation to be on the committee was to prevent change. Unfortunately, her behavior thwarted the committee's efforts, stalled the organization, and cost valuable resources—in terms of time, money, and heartache.

Authenticity Is . . .

The previous example illustrates the antithesis of authenticity. Authenticity is about being honest and consistent. In the example, the woman would say one thing and mean something else. Even worse, she would say one thing (for example, she said she wanted to be a part of the committee to help foster change) and do the opposite (she worked to prevent the changes by constantly raising objections).

To be authentic means to do what you say you will do. Emotionally intelligent leadership is also about being authentic. Here are some ways to develop your authenticity. If you're responsible for others, or to others, then they are counting on you. If you make a promise, follow through on it. If you say you value teamwork, then include others in your efforts. If you say that you will call someone, make sure that you do. With authenticity, every little action counts. The old cliché "a promise is a promise" holds profoundly true.

It's a person who isn't afraid to go against the norms to make a change. They believe in themselves, and in society as a whole, they believe that change is possible, if we only band together and use our power.
—*Female freshman at Baldwin-Wallace College, involved in an honor society, psychology club, and the wind ensemble*

Underlying authenticity is trustworthiness. Do your actions match your values? Can you be trusted? Trust is built over time, and it accumulates. Leadership exists because of a relationship among people. This relationship is strongest when trust is high. Based on what you say and what you do, you build your ability to be counted on by others. You create a sense of credibility.

Just as easily as it accumulates, however, trust can be shattered with one bad decision, action, or comment. So watch your words and your actions—they matter. One of the great challenges of leadership is to hold true to your values and do the right thing, even if no one is looking. When this happens, authenticity is at its highest.

Student Voice

"An authentic leader is willing to step back and be a follower when it is needed. They don't always need to be in charge but

when the moment arises where they need to be, they will."
—*Female sophomore at Michigan Technological University, involved in the residence hall association and a religious organization*

"Hard work, dedication, determination, and social skills are authentic enough and probably go further than any other ability. I was originally going to say the first three, but I really think the social element has to be at the top as well. Not just the ability to converse, but the ability to empathize with the experiences of others."—*Male fifth-year senior at The Ohio State University, involved in a fraternity, student government, and a job/internship*

Reflection Questions

- If you were asked to rate yourself on a scale of 1 to 10, with 10 being the highest, how authentic would you say you are? Would others rate you the same? Why or why not?
- What does it mean to be transparent in word and deed?
- When you think of authentic leaders, who comes to mind? What do they do to demonstrate authenticity?

9

FLEXIBILITY

Being Open and Adaptive to Changing Situations

According to Dictionary.com, *flexibility* means "being responsive to change; adaptability." When applied to leadership, we define flexibility as being open and adaptive to changing situations. Think of a leader or organization that exemplifies this capacity to you. Apple Computer comes to mind. Apple and its CEO Steve Jobs consistently display flexibility in product offerings and in overall business approach—often based on the needs and desires of consumers. Apple's ability to adapt has kept it afloat in an industry in constant flux. Apple's ability to create innovative products such as the iPod and the iLife series of digital media tools has set it apart from its competitors.

The Opposite of Flexibility?

Now think of individuals or organizations that are rigid or inflexible. If you are thinking of people, think of how they can get in their own way. Sometimes they do so through force. Sometimes they get their way, leaving others feeling like their ideas were not heard. Followers may comply with the course of action but are not committed to it.

A Recipe for Success

For leaders to create commitment among followers, they have to pay attention to what matters to the followers. Flexibility is a key ingredient of successful leadership. Leaders who are flexible are more likely to seek and use feedback from others. When others feel that their feedback is taken into consideration, they are more likely to support the final outcome or decision. Even if the followers' course of action is not always chosen, at least they feel heard.

Feedback often yields better solutions. After all, everyone sees issues, problems, and challenges from different vantage points. It is unlikely that one person has all the answers and perspectives! Working together achieves a better solution. Remember the story in Chapter Four about Jim and his emotional self-perception?

Flexibility can also lead to the leader being too flexible to the point of compromising the original project or goals to be accommodating to someone or something else. *Flexibility* is a slippery slope, and it's a difficult climb back up.
—*Female freshman at Baldwin-Wallace College, involved in an honor society, psychology club, and the wind ensemble*

Finally, feedback allows leaders to be more in tune with the feelings, desires, and hopes of those they serve. Consider this quote from the Chinese text *Tao Te Ching*: "Whatever is flexible and flowing will tend to grow, whatever is rigid and blocked will wither and die." Leaders who are open to possibilities and new ways of working are more likely to stay ahead of the curve. Of course, this concept can be taken to extremes and become a detriment. A leader who is too flexible will face challenges as well. Remember teachers or coaches you had who were too rigid? What about the pushovers? What opportunities did they miss? Emotionally intelligent leadership is about matching capacities with the context.

Our world is too complex to think that one way is the only right way. In today's global society there are few absolutes in terms of exercising leadership. For many years, leadership guru Ken Blanchard (1991) has discussed the necessity of changing styles depending on the situation; this is known as situational leadership. According to Northouse (2002), "effective leadership occurs when the leader can accurately diagnose the development level of subordinates in a task situation and then exhibit the prescribed leadership style that matches that situation" (p. 73).

Flexibility, rooted in a foundation of ethical principles and citizenship, is an important capacity of emotionally intelligent leadership. At times people mistake flexibility for being wishy-washy or two-faced. President Thomas Jefferson provided great guidance when he said, "In matters of style, swim with the current; in matters of principle, stand like a rock." Your ability to swim in many currents will likely determine your level of success. Your ability to remain rooted in your principles (as long as they are ethical) will keep you there.

> *Flexibility* equals versatility in many cases, and allows a leader to move with ease from one group to another.
> —*Female freshman, at University of Wisconsin–Sheboygan*

Lack of flexibility has real consequences for organizations, businesses, sports teams, and social movements. Legendary basketball coach Bobby Knight is known for his talent with the technical aspects of coaching basketball. However, his lack of flexibility—namely, his inability or refusal to align his style with the players or context—ultimately forced the decision makers at Indiana University to remove him. Many in the state of Indiana idolized Knight, yet his legacy and abilities are tarnished because of his well-known stubbornness (http://espn.go.com/ncb/news/2000/0908/729705.html). While the context was changing around Bobby Knight, he chose (at times) not to change with it.

Sometimes leaders rely on a skill set or approach that does not foster success. This is often the result of their inability to "swim with the current" as Jefferson suggested.

Student Voice

"If something doesn't go the way it was planned, it is no time to panic and break down. A little flexibility in the schedule can be a good thing. It can be a problem if you try to be flexible to accommodate everyone."—*Female junior at The Ohio State University, involved in a sorority, athletics, volunteer work, and job/internship*

"Flexibility can enhance a leader's work because it allows leaders to change a person's assignment based on their personal abilities and interests."—*Female senior at MIT, involved in an honor society, volunteer work, job/internship, and a religious organization*

"Flexibility allows for creativity. I've seen leaders who have had staff or hired help not show up or quit on them, and they've had to adapt and shuffle things around to get the job done. Such adaptation and *flexibility* to go with the flow and do what has to be done to accomplish their goal can be very beneficial to a leader."—*Male sophomore at Michigan Technological University, involved in the university programming board, a fraternity, volunteer work, and a job/internship*

"Flexibility becomes a problem when the leader stops planning concrete agendas and itineraries for programs and such. When they begin to rely on someone else to fill in the blanks and for things to simply fall together, they can get caught and be left in a bind."—*Male fifth-year senior at The Ohio State University, involved in a fraternity, student government, and a job/internship*

"It is a wonderful thing for a leader to be flexible; in fact, that's part of leadership. An effective leader must expect the unexpected, and be prepared for the most unusual circumstances."—*Female freshman at Baldwin-Wallace College, involved in an honor society, psychology club, and the wind ensemble*

Reflection Questions

- Do your peers see you as flexible or rigid in style? In what way or ways?
- How does this perception help or hurt you in different situations?
- Flexibility must rest on a foundation of ethics and principles. What principles serve as your foundation?

10

ACHIEVEMENT

Being Driven to Improve According to Personal Standards

For EIL, the definition of achievement is "being driven to improve according to personal standards." Many of us know *achievement* when we see and feel it. For what do you have a passion? A musical instrument? A hobby or form of art? A sport? No matter what an emotionally intelligent leader's passion is, the leader will pursue it to a high level of achievement and inspire those around them to work at increased levels as well.

Passion + Flow = Success

It is important for leaders to examine what it is they feel passionate about. Passion is an energy source unlike any other. A passion put into action is sometimes called flow (Csikszentmihalyi, 1990). In essence, flow is a psychological state you enter when you lose track of time. Can you think of an activity you love so much that you completely lose track of time when you do it? For some it is dance or writing; for others it is a video game or hobby. When you love doing something, it is not difficult to enter the state of flow.

> Achievement is relative. Too often do we fall into this paradigm that achievement is measured by grades and a résumé? A person is achieving at a satisfactory level when, at the end of each day, they can sit down and ask themselves the questions: Was I productive today? Am I satisfied with what I did today?
> —*Male junior at Miami University (Ohio), involved in a fraternity, honor society, student government, residence hall association, volunteer work, job/internship, and athletics*

Flow also fosters achievement. Do you think it is difficult for Tiger Woods to motivate himself to play golf? Perhaps some days, but many would agree that he was placed on earth to play golf. It just "clicks" for him. How about Christina Aguilera, Leonardo DiCaprio, or Maya Angelou? All of them seem to be doing what they love and what they have a passion for. As a result, achievement is not difficult.

To boil this concept down, think back to high school for a moment. Which topics did you like? Math? English? Gym? Most likely you were much more successful in the class or classes that just "clicked" for you. In these classes, achieving was probably not a challenge—it probably took less effort and time than those classes you did not enjoy. In those cases you experienced flow.

Achievement and Leadership

So what does this have to do with leadership? First, you should get involved in organizations you feel passionate about. If you are involved for other reasons, like power or status, it is possible you are doing yourself and the organization a disservice. For instance, some people choose a profession because they can make a lot of money, not because they truly believe in the profession. Unless money truly is your passion, it won't buy happiness. For many, all the money in the world cannot offset the misery that results from the feeling of being stuck at a job that is uninspiring, unsatisfying, or downright miserable.

The Efficient Way to Success

In many ways, placing your efforts in areas for which you feel great passion is the quickest and most efficient way to succeed. At the same time, we all have to work occasionally on activities that we do not enjoy. After all, that is part of the process of meeting our goals. However, when people are doing what they love, they're motivated to succeed, feel energized by the work itself, and feel inspired.

A wonderful way to give back to your organization is to help others discover which aspects of the organization for which they have a passion. If those around you love their roles within the organization, it will not seem like work. It will be fun and feel more like a hobby. Mark Twain said, "Make your vocation your vacation." All too often people do not follow their passion and core purpose, which makes achievement more of a challenge. With passion as a part of your foundation, you have an amazing starting point from which to begin the journey.

Student Voice

"Achievement is achieving something without sacrificing values and emotional health."—*Male senior at* The Catholic University of America, *involved in student government, a fraternity, volunteer work, and orientation*

"Achievement is students who can say they take pride in their work and are able to make a positive contribution to their campus through activities and organizations."—*Female junior at Michigan Technological University, involved in the residence hall association, a professional organization, athletics, job/internship, and a religious organization*

"I think a healthy level of achievement (or success) helps build a healthy self-esteem within a person. The joy of achieving something also can then drive an individual to further achievement." —*Male fifth-year senior at* The Ohio State University, *involved in a fraternity, student government, and a job/internship*

Reflection Questions

- What activities, topics, sports, or hobbies bring you into the psychological state of "flow"?

- Have you ever lost your love for a game or activity? What happened to your level of achievement?

- What are your personal thoughts about achievement? What have we missed?

11

OPTIMISM

Being Positive

Emotionally intelligent leadership includes a healthy positive outlook and displaying a positive regard for the future. The authors of *The Leadership Challenge*, Kouzes and Posner (2007), might call this "inspiring a shared vision." Optimism is a powerful force that many of us overlook. However, research has found that being optimistic is an important element of emotional intelligence and leadership (Avolio & Luthans, 2006; Goleman, Boyatzis, & McKee, 2002).

> When optimism is streaming through an organization, there is no end to the possibilities that could be accomplished. There is thought, creativity, relaxation, and, most of all, fun.
> —*Male sophomore at Michigan Technological University, involved in the university programming board, fraternity, volunteer, job/internship*

Visualizing the Two Extremes

Think about the place where you get or renew your driver's license, and then think about your favorite coffee shop. Where would you rather spend your time? More often than not, the place where you get your driver's license is a place likely filled with staff and customers who do not want to be there. Your favorite coffee shop, on the other hand, is likely filled with staff and customers happy to be there.

Most likely, the coffee shop is a place where you feel welcome, where you see familiar faces, and where you feel good about taking your business. When you think about the place where you renew your driver's license, we imagine many of you may leave feeling frustrated. Thinking about the coffee shop, however, should fill you with positive thoughts and feelings. You are then more likely to feel optimistic and be able to create a sense of optimism among others.

Another way to visualize what optimism entails is to think back to a recent group project. Think of the group members who showed up to meetings and were willing to take on various components of the task. They may very well have been challenging to work with because they were so motivated or engaged, but chances are they also kept a positive attitude about finishing the project and wanting to do well. Perhaps you felt they made the best of the situation.

It is likely that you've also worked on a group project in which some of the group members were difficult to work with. They were either apathetic or showed up late or had a bad attitude about everything. Did they energize you? Did you feel excited and eager to get to work on the tasks at hand? We imagine working with these people was more of a challenge.

With optimism, you see the possibilities, you search for opportunities to do more or learn more. Emotions are contagious. Would you rather catch a positive flow of energy or a negative flow?

What kind of person are you? Do people enjoy working with you? Do you find people choosing to spend time with you? Are you a positive influence on the organization or an energy drain? These questions can help you identify your attitude and abilities as they relate to optimism.

Realistic Optimism

Optimistic people are not oblivious to real issues. Optimistic people see complexities and problems as inherent in all organizations. However, optimism leads them to approach situations and relationships in a different manner. Emotionally intelligent leaders understand that challenges are part of the game, and they work with others to move past them without dwelling on the negatives. They know how to see the possibilities without ignoring the realities.

> Optimism is, often times, great for organizations, groups, teams, and offices. However, sometimes too much optimism turns people away.
> —*Female sophomore at University of Wisconsin–Sheboygan, involved in volunteer work and a job/internship*

In addition, those who are optimistic help others to see possibilities. For example, optimism helps us see conflict as a catalyst for deepening or strengthening a relationship, rather than as the end of a relationship. Optimism helps us identify gaps or weaknesses and turn them into learning opportunities or even assets. Emotionally intelligent leaders capitalize on untapped potential, unleash an energy similar to flow, adapt to where the collective energy exists, and use optimism to their advantage.

Contagious Emotions

Research supports the benefits of an optimistic point of view. For example, a business concept called "mood linkage" explains instances in which the mood or outlook of an individual or small group affects the entire organization (Williams, 2005). This concept can work for or against you.

Think of an organization or sports team with great success. The team members seem to be on a collective high. Now think back to a time when you were in an organization in which the leader or a small group of influential individuals was negative toward the organization. You may have heard comments such as "Things used to be so much better"; "This organization is going nowhere"; "The current leadership is going to drive it into the ground"; "I don't care anymore—I could care less." If left unattended or unaddressed, these comments are poisonous to an organization.

So what type of leader are you? Would people in your organization view you as optimistic or pessimistic? Do people enjoy being around you? Are everyday challenges huge issues that get you down or do you navigate these hurdles with ease and grace? What would those who know you best say?

Ask your mentors or more experienced people in your organization about optimism. They have probably spent years working or associating with people who are negative and draining. Ask your parents or friends to share characteristics of negative people. Ask them how they react to negativity. What suggestions do they have for you in the event that you encounter similar people?

Conclusion

Some people seem innately optimistic; others tend to look on the negative side. If you find it hard to see the positive or to be optimistic, try spending time with people who you believe are optimistic. Learn from their examples. Begin to develop that part of you that appreciates people or things more. As you focus on developing more appreciation, you'll begin to shift your thinking more toward the positive. Although optimism may not become your greatest strength, it can become a skill set to use throughout your life.

Student Voice

"Optimism is huge. When a group or leader gets excited, others tend to follow suit, and soon a positive aura surrounds them." —*Male senior at Case Western Reserve University, involved in athletics, an honor society, job/internship, and volunteer work*

———

"Optimism is a key ingredient to leadership. An optimistic leader has the ability to inspire followers, gain trust and support, and work to make a positive impact on people. Optimism is necessary for a successful endeavor."—*Female freshman at Baldwin-Wallace*

College, involved in an honor society, a job/internship, psychology club, and the wind ensemble

Reflection Questions

- How have you seen optimism affect organizations? How does a lack of optimism affect others?
- Can you think of a time when optimism became a detriment to a leader?
- On a scale of 1 to 10, with 10 being highest, at what level of optimism would you rate the organization with which you most closely associate? On what basis do you make this rating?

12

INITIATIVE

Wanting and Seeking Opportunities

What if Abraham Lincoln had not taken the initiative to tackle slavery in the United States? What if he had decided that it was simply too controversial to take on? All of us would be different people, living in a different world. Leaders such as Mahatma Gandhi, Nelson Mandela, Gloria Steinem, Susan B. Anthony, Martin Luther King Jr., Golda Meir, Mikhail Gorbachev, Mother Theresa, and Lech Walesa have embodied change in their countries and the world. Each of these great individuals took initiative, even when faced with seemingly insurmountable odds.

Emotionally intelligent leaders understand and take initiative. We define this type of initiative as being assertive in seeking opportunities. Assertiveness is key because the individuals just listed not only saw that the world could be different, but they also took action. In his video *The Power of Vision* (1991), futurist Joel Barker suggests, "Vision without action is merely a dream. Action without vision just passes time. Vision with action changes the world."

The Hallmarks of Initiative

So what does initiative look like? First, those with initiative seek people and resources to assist them along their journey or with their project or ideas. They understand the inherent obstacles in their work and realize that to overcome them they will use their resources to climb under, crawl over, and work through barriers in an ethical, entrepreneurial manner.

A second hallmark of those with initiative is that they always seem to be ahead of the curve. Think about Madonna and her music career—for years she has been widely perceived to be on the cutting edge of pop culture, often because of some risks that she took in terms of her lyrics, her dancing, and even what she wore. Successful designers, architects, programmers, video game architects, artists, musicians, and others are constantly thinking about the "next big thing." Think of someone in your organization who is innovative or an entrepreneurial thinker. What is it about these individuals that shows initiative?

A third hallmark of those with initiative is that they have a passion for what they are doing. In this respect, initiative links directly to *achievement*. Emotionally intelligent leaders know that they can make change happen—maybe even make their group or the world a better place. Abraham Lincoln gave his life for a cause he believed in (as did many others in the American Civil War). He used his position to right a wrong that had existed in the United States for years.

> Students who take initiative tend to be the students who see positive results in a relatively small amount of time.
> —*Female junior at The Catholic University of America, involved in a sorority, student government, residence hall association, athletics, volunteer work, and a religious organization*

A fourth hallmark of initiative is laser-like focus. Initiative requires you to set a goal and stay focused on the end product. With this focus, you are highly motivated and not easily distracted until you have met your goal. You may get up early, stay late, and view everything through the lens of meeting your goals and the goals of the group or organization.

Conclusion

Emotionally intelligent leaders find opportunities. They seek them out and stay focused on them. Hearing the words "no" or "I'm sorry, this won't work" doesn't mean much to the emotionally intelligent leader. Nor will an emotionally intelligent leader be content to wait and see what happens. Initiative means that when emotionally intelligent leaders discover a closed door, they see it as just that—a closed door, waiting to be opened. Many other doors are waiting to be opened. With initiative, we know this to be true.

Student Voice

"Student initiative can be seen all the time. My view (getting ready to graduate) is a lot more holistic than it once was. From the fraternity brother working twenty hours while going to school, to the student who dedicates many hours a week to volunteering, these are all initiative in my mind. What still baffles me is the sense of no initiative that is exhibited by the 80 percent we often talk about."— *Male fifth-year senior at The Ohio State University, involved in a fraternity, student government, and a job/internship*

"Recently I watched a particular group member stand back and realize what the others had done or already were doing. She did her best to pick off the remaining assignments to help get things done better and faster."—*Female fifth-year senior at Florida State University, involved in a sorority and a job/internship*

"A great example is when a friend of mine, who is a business student and RA, organized a hall social event with a retail store. The store gave everyone in the hall a 15 percent discount and kept the store open late for them, and the store got around $500 in sales in one hour."—*Male junior at Michigan Technological University, involved in a professional organization, athletics, assistant teacher, and a religious organization*

"Initiative comes in many forms. Sometimes it is as simple as doing your homework, but more often it is expressed through stepping up to the plate and taking on a task that no one else will. This can be planning an event, confronting someone, or speaking out for an ideal. Initiative can sometimes motivate others as well."—*Male senior at University of Cincinnati, involved in a fraternity, honor society, professional organization, and a job/internship*

Reflection Questions

- What is it like to work with a leader who displays a low level of initiative? A high level of initiative?
- What effect can a low level of initiative have on an organization?
- What does extreme initiative look like? Can it hurt an organization? If so, how?

Part Three

CONSCIOUSNESS OF OTHERS

Being Aware of Your Relationship with Others and the Role They Play in the Leadership Equation

Empathy

Citizenship

Inspiration

Influence

Coaching

Change Agent

Conflict Management

Developing Relationships

Teamwork

Capitalizing on Difference

Consciousness of others means that emotionally intelligent leaders are aware of and attuned to those with whom they are working. As you know, followers are a major and integral component of the leadership equation. The role of others must be taken into consideration for emotionally intelligent leadership to occur.

Consciousness of others includes a person's ability to empathize, inspire, influence, coach, manage conflict, and effect change. All of these involve working with other people. The challenge is this: because the context (socioeconomic status, country, organization) changes so often, there is an infinite number of variables affecting leadership. As a result, you need to work with others to clarify their dreams, aspirations, work styles, communication patterns, and so forth.

For instance, Scott recently had a conversation with his sister, who said that she appreciated a leader who took command, didn't get caught up in the day-to-day niceties of work, and took a direct approach with her. This desire may fly in the face of many current models of leadership; however, this style of leadership works for her, which cannot be discounted. After all, if her boss hopes to get the best from her, he must adapt his style to meet her needs. Other coworkers in the same area may despise the idea of a leader barking orders at them. So as a leader do you influence, empathize, inspire, direct, or coach others? In many cases the answer is, it depends. One critical task of the leader is to ask the right questions and find out what others need and want, then strive to provide it.

Effective leadership is like being on a golf course and using the right golf clubs well in the right situation. The best players have mastered this technique. They are aware of how the weather, the course, and the competition contribute to the equation. The best players have the skills to choose intentionally and play effectively with different clubs, given new or changing circumstances.

What "leadership clubs" do you use well? The "authoritative club"? The "friend club"? The "facilitation club"? The "controlling club"? The "motivating club"? Which clubs do you not use well? Are you great at coming up with big ideas but challenged by implementing them? Knowing yourself well enough to know this means that you can better equip yourself to be surrounded by others who are great in follow-through, or at least good in areas in which you are not. You and those around you need to master a number of "leadership clubs." In so doing, you will adapt better to the needs and expectations of others. And you will be more effective in demonstrating your emotionally intelligent leadership.

13

EMPATHY

Understanding Others from
Their Perspective

Empathy is one of the most powerful and difficult EIL capacities to learn and practice. Perceiving the emotions of others enables us to build healthier relation-

> Empathy allows a leader to understand the lives of those people he or she is leading.
> —*Male senior at University of Nebraska–Lincoln, involved in a fraternity, honor society, professional organization, volunteer work, job/internship, and a religious organization*

ships, manage difficult situations, and develop trust more effectively. Being empathetic requires you to have a high level of self-awareness as well as awareness of others. To be empathetic you must know what you are feeling in order to acknowledge and identify what others may be feeling. With this as your foundation, you can put yourself in someone else's shoes. To do this, you must be perceptive and sensitive to what you see, hear, and think.

Listening with Empathy

One way to move empathy from an intangible idea to a practical skill is to think about empathy in the context of communication. For example, when you listen empathetically, you hear people's words using your ears, eyes, and heart. Translation? You hear their words along with *how* those words are spoken. You listen for the tone used. You pay attention to body language. You focus on what they are saying, not on what you want to say back. Stephen Covey (1989) identifies this concept as one of his *Seven Habits of Highly Effective People*—"seek first to understand, then be understood" (p. 237).

Demonstrating Empathy

Showing empathy is not easy. You may feel empathetic, yet some might say that this capacity is in the eyes of the beholder. Empathy expressed by one person may not be perceived by another. This means that you have to practice your skills and learn how others think you effectively display empathy. Ask for feedback from others you trust. Would they say you're empathetic? How well are you listening empathetically? What are you saying to someone else with your body language? Are you communicating openness and interest in what someone is saying? If someone is telling you something, are you looking around or sitting in a way that says "Whatever"? If this is true, no matter what you say, you may not be perceived as being empathetic.

Involving Your Heart

Demonstrating empathy for another comes from your heart and not your head. It's not just about saying the right words. Being empathetic means sincerely feeling that what you're saying communicates your thoughts and your feelings appropriately. Think about a difficult time in your life. Who did you feel was there for you? Was it a friend, parent, teacher, or coach? How did you know you had this person's support? What did this person do?

In summary, empathy means that you feel with another person. You understand people's experiences and feelings from their perspectives, not your own. Empathy is different from sympathy; sympathy means "putting yourself in another person's place but retaining your own perspective and still using your own standard of judgment" (Komives, Lucas, & McMahon, 2007, p. 171). Sympathy involves pity; empathy requires understanding. And understanding requires your heart and mind to be connected. With empathy, your consciousness of self connects with your consciousness with others as a result of your consciousness of context.

Student Voice

"Empathy is one of the most important abilities of a leader. Empathy, by my definition, is the ability to understand what people feel (and why they feel that way). By contrast, sympathy is feeling what a person feels along with her. Empathy is important for leaders because understanding the motivations of other people can only help the leader improve a team."—*Female senior at MIT, involved in an honor society, volunteer work, job/internship, and a religious organization*

"Too much empathy will slow the group down tremendously. A leader can't make everyone happy. Everyone should be heard and feedback should be given when the wrong or impossible ideas or opinions are shared."—*Female senior at University of Iowa, involved in a job/internship and as a peer writing tutor*

"When a leader is in balance with empathy, then ideas are received and the members of that group can leave at the end of the day knowing that they contributed something to the cause."—*Male sophomore at Michigan Technological University, involved in a fraternity, university programming board, volunteer work, and a job/internship*

Reflection Questions

- How important is empathy to leadership? Would you consider it an essential skill? Why or why not?
- How does empathy or the lack of it affect the relationship between leaders and followers?

14

CITIZENSHIP

Recognizing and Fulfilling Your
Responsibility for Others or the Group

Is your organization, workplace, or social group made up of good citizens? What does it mean to be a good citizen in your organization? Your school? Your community? Your country? Many qualities of a good citizen are socially constructed. In other words, the definition of a good citizen at a Catholic university may be different from the definition at a small private liberal arts college. Being a good citizen in Beijing may look different from being a good citizen in Dallas. Citizenship depends on context.

Citizenship and Leadership

So how does the concept of citizenship relate to emotionally intelligent leadership? First, you must be aware of what it means to be a good citizen in an organization. "To be a good citizen is to work for positive change on behalf of others and the community" (Higher Education Research Institute, 1996, p. 23). For instance, if you are in a fraternity or sorority, it means that you attend meetings, pay your bills, support one another through good times and bad, participate in philanthropy events, and give back as an alumnus. If you are a member of an athletic team, you must show up to practice on time, respond to the coach's instructions, challenge and support each other, and be committed to your sport and fellow team members. As part of any sort of commitment, there are expectations that you be a good citizen.

> People are more likely to believe in a person and respect someone who recognizes and fulfills responsibilities to others. People are also more likely to follow such a leader because they believe this person to be someone who truly has an interest in the people, and can be trusted.
>
> —*Female freshman at University of Wisconsin–Sheboygan*

Citizenship also implies an important larger concept. Citizens understand they are part of something bigger than themselves. Interdependence is recognized as a reality of life in organizations and groups (Higher Education Research Institute, 1996). Because of this, citizens must give of themselves for the benefit of others. When individuals agree to join or serve in leadership positions, they commit to the values, rules, goals, and mission of the organization. Sometimes this means making personal sacrifices for the good of the group or even just one member. They move beyond self-interest when they demonstrate citizenship.

The challenge is this: often leaders and members have little recognition of what it means to be good citizens of their organization. This is no one's fault per se. In contrast, emotionally intelligent leaders are acutely aware of what it means to be good citizens. They do their best to fall in line with expectations. They model the way, do what they say they will do, and embody the values of the organization (Kouzes & Posner, 2007).

An Organizational Scan

Is your organization filled with good citizens or apathetic members? Are there people who want to take the organization to the next level or are members content with the status quo? Almost all organizations have three or four people who do a lot; however, not many organizations are filled with a majority of good citizens. Part of the job of an emotionally intelligent leader is to fill the organization with as many good citizens as possible and to hold everyone accountable to a set of standards.

In most organizations there is a great deal of untapped potential. The current culture of your organization may enable apathy or disrespect to some degree. When this happens, and good citizenship doesn't exist, potential is lost and individuals and organizations flounder. However, in an organization filled with good citizens, a different reality is possible—one in which everyone is respected and appreciated, in which someone has taken the time to tap those individuals and have one-on-one conversations to increase motivation and involvement.

Student Voice

"I believe that there comes a point in an individual's life where they realize that satisfaction does not simply result from making yourself happy. It results from interactions with others and fulfilling their needs. When this occurs, a group runs more efficiently." —*Female senior at Michigan Technological University, involved in an honor society, professional organization, and a job/internship*

"When members fulfill their duty, the entire aura of the organization is positive. Those not fulfilling duties feel guilty for such, and then rise to the level of responsibility of others."—*Male junior at Miami University* (Ohio)

"When someone fulfills their responsibility, a group works very well. Oftentimes this person can go unnoticed, in which case it's the leader's responsibility to recognize their efforts and acknowledge them for their good work."—*Male sophomore at Florida State University, involved in the university programming board, residence hall association, and volunteer work*

Reflection Questions

- What does it mean to be a good citizen in your organization? Would others agree with your definition?

- What happens when an individual does not model good citizenship? What can this do to the organization?

- What if the organization is too rigid in its definition of a good citizen? Can you name an example in which the definition may have actually hindered progress? Think both historically and in terms of modern life.

15

INSPIRATION

Motivating and Moving Others Toward a Shared Vision

In general, academic scholars cannot agree on a common definition of leadership. In his book *Leadership*, James MacGregor Burns says, "leadership is one of the most observed yet least understood phenomena on earth" (1978, p. 2). In other words, we know it when we see it, and we know it when we feel it; however, what "it" actually is can be challenging to describe or define. After all, in many ways leadership is in the eye of the beholder. Someone who is inspirational to one person is not necessarily inspirational to another. To some in World War II, Joseph Stalin was a leader. For others, Winston Churchill was a leader. It all depends on one's vantage point. We do not view Stalin as a great leader but we acknowledge that, to many, he was.

The "It" Factor

Inspiration is defined as that which motivates and moves others toward a shared vision. The inspirational motivation dimension is produced through behaviors that generate a feeling of optimism and a commitment to organizational goals and vision. Influential leaders often generate this optimism and commitment by communicating their ideals and vision for the organization (Bass, 1985). Emotionally intelligent leaders are in tune with the values of their followers. They are aware of the context in which they find themselves and have the ability to influence those around them. People follow their lead and commit to the direction in which the leaders want to take the organization or movement. People choose to follow inspirational leaders.

We hope that by this point in the book you better understand why leaders have the ability to inspire. People support what they help to create. When people feel a part of an organization, movement, or organizational direction, they have "it" in their heart. They feel committed to the cause or a course of action.

> By being included, I will want to contribute more. If I feel like an outsider, I would not want to come to the meetings or activities, and I would eventually become disinterested in the group.
> —*Female sophomore at Appalachian State University, involved in a religious organization*

When was the last time you felt committed to a cause or course of action? On a sports team? With a group of friends? Working with your church, synagogue, or mosque? Volunteering for an organization that means a great deal to you? Most of us know the feeling. The important point for all of us to think through is what made us feel this way. Was it our peers or coworkers? Was it a leader? Was it the cause? Was it the vision? Was it a combination of many factors? Regardless, leaders should be aware of these factors in themselves and in those who follow. Because leadership exists in the eye of the beholder, emotionally intelligent leaders ask—rather than guess—what followers value and what the organization values.

Inspirational Leadership

To informally develop your capacity for inspiration, ask a few people you like, admire, and respect what they want or need from a leader. You can learn a lot from these conversations. Consider questions such as these:

- What do I need to do to be effective in this role?
- How can I improve over what past leaders have done?
- Where does the organization need to focus its efforts?
- What inspires or motivates you?

The more you ask, the more you learn. The more you learn, the better prepared you are to lead. All too often, leaders think they know what their own blind spots are, what others want, and how others feel. After advising and working with students and student organizations for more than a decade, we know firsthand that this is not always the case. Research supports the importance of receiving feedback and learning from what others see (Avolio & Luthans, 2006).

What inspires me as a follower is seeing a leader jump into the pit with you to dig the organization out of the hole they have made.
—*Male senior at University of Cincinnati, involved in a fraternity, honor society, professional organization, job/ internship, and volunteer work*

In many respects, the best way to inspire others is to make them feel heard and valued. Inspiring others includes caring about them, their interests, their successes, and where they fit into the organization. It means showing them that you understand what they need and want. Although you can't be all things to all people, you must know those whom you are leading and what makes them tick. Think of those people along the way who have done this for you. That is another great way to improve your understanding of inspiration.

Student Voice

"As a follower, I like someone who will give me specific tasks and guide me, but not try to control exactly what I do. I like to be given something specific but still like to have the creative freedom to do what I think is best with it. As a follower, I like someone who will respect what I do, and truly value my opinion."—*Female junior at University of Iowa, involved in an honor society, volunteer work, and a job/internship*

"I enjoy honesty and consistency. A leader who upholds themselves in a manner that I aspire to is an inspiration to me."—*Male junior at Miami University (Ohio), involved in a fraternity, honor society, student government, residence hall association, volunteer work, job/internship, and athletics*

"I like leaders who are visionary (have good ideas), optimistic (believe something can get done), and encouraging (appreciate the contributions of the different teammates). These sorts of leaders make me want to follow them."—*Female senior at MIT, involved in an honor society, volunteer work, job/internship, and a religious organization*

Reflection Questions

- What qualities do you find in an inspirational leader? Ask your best friend the same question. Ask your parents and grandparents. Ask someone from a different culture. What are the similarities and differences?

- Do you consider yourself inspirational? If so, in what way(s)? What makes other people feel this way about you? If not, what do you need to change?

- How do you know what is inspiring others? How do you know what others are looking for in a leader?

16

INFLUENCE

Demonstrating Skills of Persuasion

Effective leaders have the ability to influence those around them. You see it all the time. Sit in a park and watch a group of kids play on the playground for thirty minutes. Some children consistently have the ability to encourage and influence others to play what they want to play—sometimes through words, other times through force. For most of us, the days of hitting another person when we don't get our way are over—at least we hope they are! What's left are your words and actions.

Power as Influence

Bass (1997) suggests that "leaders display conviction; emphasize trust; take stands on different issues; present their most important values; emphasize the importance of purpose, commitment and ethical consequences of decision making. Such leaders are admired as role models in generating pride, loyalty, confidence, and alignment around a shared purpose" (p. 133). Influence is a form of power, so it is important to know how people gain and lose power in organizations. In his book *Leadership in Organizations*, Gary Yukl (2002) discusses five primary kinds of power:

- *Reward power:* When a person has the ability to influence others because of the ability to reward others for a job well done
- *Coercive power:* When a person has the ability to influence others through the ability to punish those who do not fall in line

- *Legitimate power:* When a person requests a course of action from others and those being asked comply out of an obligation to the leader of the organization
- *Expert power:* When a person has the ability to influence others through knowledge or experience as it applies to the organization or field
- *Referent power:* When a person has the ability to influence others because of the admiration or respect offered by followers

Read these again and think of someone who uses each of these kinds of power to influence others around them. Based on your experience, which kinds of power work? Which do you connect with? How are you motivated? What works for those you know? Is it the same for others in your organization?

> Leaders that are understanding (don't expect me to do more work than I am able) and fair (treating me according to my needs) influence me to keep working for them.
> —*Female senior at MIT, involved in an honor society, volunteer work, job/internship and a religious organization*

Keeping in mind these definitions of power, let's turn to the concept of influence. To us, this means that an individual can demonstrate skills of persuasion. In other words, influence is about having the ability to gain buy-in from others. Influential people are often admired and respected. In some way they symbolize or embody organizational values. These individuals "walk the walk." Their actions are in sync with their words. Their behavior fosters a sense of confidence and trust in their followers, organizations, or friends.

Case in Point: Oprah Winfrey

It has been widely discussed in management texts and the media that Oprah Winfrey is one of the most admired and successful business people in recent history. She is a media mogul, and when we look closely at how she has gained her power, we see that it is in large part through her ability to influence her viewers. Many who know and watch Oprah describe her as real and down to earth. She portrays (and we assume is) a transparent and authentic person to all around her. In other words, who she is on screen and who she is off screen are congruent.

This style has gained Oprah a great deal of influence and power in her industry as well as in society at large. When Oprah recommends a book to her viewers, it becomes an instant best-seller. When she highlights a product or resource, people investigate it and purchase it in droves. She has earned this power and influence over years of consistent and authentic behavior.

Two key words in the preceding sentence are *consistent* and *years*. Many people today are skeptical of leaders. Research shows that there is little trust of industry and governmental leaders (Avolio & Luthans, 2006). Long gone are the days when leaders are blindly trusted simply because of their positions or titles. Followers have been hurt too often. To succeed, have influence, and gain power in organizations, you need to embody the organization's values or the values of others, in your words and actions, as consistently as possible. You need to develop meaningful relationships with others who can help make a shared vision reality. Becoming influential takes time and hard work, but being influential is a solid attribute of any leader, on campus or in the community.

Student Voice

"I'm influenced by a leader who is intelligent and charismatic, a leader who takes time to understand me as a follower and explains each and every action."—*Male junior at Miami University (Ohio)*

"When someone is too strong and too demanding. . . it influences me to not want to work with them."—*Female sophomore at Michigan Technological University, involved in a residence hall association and a religious organization*

"The same hands-on style influences me as a follower. When I see the leader doing their share of work, it motivates me to pull my own weight and do what I'm supposed to do and maybe more." —*Male junior at Baldwin-Wallace College, involved in the university programming board, student government, residence hall association, and athletics*

"I need a leader who is empathetic to my situation and passionate about the cause in order to respect him."—*Female sophomore at University of Wisconsin-Sheboygan, involved in volunteer work and a job/internship*

Reflection Questions

- How have you seen an individual gain power in an organization?
- How have you seen an individual lose power in an organization?
- How does influence relate to the other capacities outlined in the model of emotionally intelligent leadership?

17

COACHING

Helping Others Enhance Their Skills and Abilities

The term *coaching* may not resonate with some of you because you may never have had a personal coach. For others, this word conjures up visions of a high school sports coach or revered professional coach. This image may foster positive or negative memories based on your experiences. Regardless of your personal experiences or impressions, consider the definition of *coach* from Dictionary.com:

(1) a person who trains or directs athletes or athletic teams; (2) a person who gives instruction, as in singing or acting; and (3) a private tutor employed to prepare a student for an examination.

We like the words *train* and *prepare* in this definition. These words help connect coaching to leadership—doing what is necessary to train and prepare others for the tasks or challenges at hand. Here's another aspect to the definition: in a leadership context, coaching also involves a willingness to learn from others. The relationship is reciprocal. The leader cannot know it all. Even the best coaches in the world consistently learn from their athletes, students, or protégés, particularly about what approaches do and do not work.

> I had a mentor who met weekly with me to discuss how the meeting went and what to do the following week.
> —*Male senior at University of Nebraska–Lincoln, involved in a fraternity, honor society, professional organization, religious organization, volunteer work, and job/internship*

A key concept related to this capacity is the idea of working *with* others toward new goals and directions. Effective coaches care about and seek feedback from those with whom they work. They work together to determine the best way to reach their goals.

Effective Leaders Are Effective Coaches

Another way to understand coaching is to look at the emerging business of executive coaching. Consultants who serve as executive coaches can make between $1,500 and $15,000 a day ("When executive coaching fails to deliver," 2003). Feel like changing your major? The International Coach Federation (www.coachfederation.com) discusses the concept of coaching:

> Professional coaching is an ongoing professional relationship that helps people produce extraordinary results in their lives, careers, businesses or organizations. Through the process of coaching, clients deepen their learning, improve their performance, and enhance their quality of life.

Unfortunately, all too often we see what could be deemed the dictatorial approach to leadership, which does not always work. Think of acquaintances who always take the "directive" or "authoritative" approach to leadership (recall our golf analogy—using different approaches like different "clubs"). What is their reputation among peers? It is likely that many people don't want to be around this style of leadership. We have found and experienced that this approach undermines the long-term effectiveness of leadership. In fact, research in emotional intelligence has concluded that the authoritative style, as well as a couple of others (coercive and pacesetting styles), "should not be relied upon exclusively, and all have short-term uses" (Goleman, 2000, p. 81). Although an authoritative style may yield desired results in the short term, in the long run it does not lead to the level of commitment, engagement, or empowerment that emotionally intelligent leadership seeks to develop.

Conclusion

In their book *Leadership and the One Minute Manager*, Blanchard, Zigarmi, and Zigarmi (1985) assert that "High directive/high supportive behavior is referred to as coaching. In this style the leader still provides a great deal of direction, but he/she also attempts to hear the employees' feelings about a decision as well as their ideas and suggestions" (p. 22).

To develop your own coaching capacity, try working with others to accomplish tasks or help others to develop their skills. Show emerging leaders the ropes. You can even develop your own coaching capacity by finding someone to show you the ropes. Keep lines of communication open, and respond to the feedback you receive. Seek new directions together, and you may be surprised at what you and others can accomplish together.

Student Voice

"I personally believed that when my organization voted me president they were taking a big leap of faith. I now realize they saw all of the deep leadership qualities in me that I only saw on the surface. This one experience and position has expanded my capabilities as a leader, and I am thankful for that."—*Female senior at Michigan Technological University, involved in a sorority, honor society, professional organization, and job/internship*

"I co-taught a religious education program for three years with a neighbor across the street. Her ability to be 'on the spot' taught me that I don't need to be so uptight and have everything structured."—*Female junior at University of Wisconsin–Sheboygan, involved in a job/internship*

"Some of the co-workers I had interacted with saw me in a very positive way, which taught me right away how to treat others, and the importance of treating others in a friendly and welcoming way."—*Male junior at Michigan Technological University, involved in a professional organization, athletics, assistant teaching, and a religious organization*

Reflection Questions

- Who are some people who have helped you along the way? Based on this chapter's explanation of coaching, would you consider them coaches? Why or why not?

- Does the concept of coaching exist in your organization? If not, what would it look like? If so, how do you experience it?

- Make an argument against the notion that "effective leaders are effective coaches."

18

CHANGE AGENT

Seeking Out and Working with Others Toward New Directions

Change is all around us. Change happens faster today than at any previous point in history. What does it mean to be a change agent? How can you understand yourself as someone who makes change happen? Should you change for change's sake? Certainly not.

Being a change agent means you look for opportunities for improvement or innovation. Changes may benefit one person, an organization, or a whole community. To be a change agent, you must possess certain skills, such as creative problem solving. In addition, you must have certain attitudes; for example, a comfort with risk taking. A change agent is also sensitive to time. For change to be effective, you must consider the timing of a change effort.

> Many times, a change that needs to be made requires someone to step up and take a stand for what is right. A lot of people are afraid to initiate changes because they do not want people to oppose them or the change to fail.
> —*Female junior at Michigan Technological University, involved in a residence hall association, professional organization, religious organizations, athletics, and a job/internship*

Challenge the Process

In *The Leadership Challenge* (2007), James Kouzes and Barry Posner write about challenging the process. Based on their research, Kouzes and Posner assert that effective leadership is all about making change happen. This brief description conveys the essence of what it means to be a change agent. There are two major components of challenging the process: looking for opportunities and taking risks (Kouzes & Posner, 2007).

Looking for Opportunities

In most organizations, groups, teams, and businesses, success depends on the leader's ability to look for opportunities. You may find opportunities as a resident assistant, in a club, on a sports team, and in the working world. Looking for opportunities may require you to find new groups with which to partner or develop new programming or business ventures.

Whatever the opportunity, we know from research what happens when leaders stop looking for it—success and effectiveness diminish. From personal stories to examples from corporate America, we see how successful leaders or companies fail when leaders assume they will always be on top. In *Good to Great*, Jim Collins (2001) found that industry leaders such as Upjohn and Bethlehem Steel lost their competitive edge, market share, and profitability when their leaders became complacent in their success. They stopped looking for opportunities.

> There needs to be the catalyst for change, and sometimes it is someone who stands above the rest and says, "let's do this" who initiates that change. Change can be scary but, when someone cries for it and gets momentum going, it is not so bad.
> —*Male sophomore at Michigan Technological University, involved in a fraternity, university programming board, volunteer work, and a job/internship*

One antidote to complacency is initiative, another EIL capacity. When you take the initiative to look for opportunities, you align yourself with a change agent who seeks out new opportunities, programs, or ventures. She or he looks for improvements in systems or processes, even if one of these is running well. For instance, a change agent in an organization might ask, "How can I run this meeting in a way that is more interesting and engaging, instead of following the usual agenda?"

Taking Risks

To make change happen, you must accept uncertainty. This takes courage and patience. In today's society, we face pressure to succeed and not make mistakes. This is particularly true for people in leadership positions. Certainty of success is in direct opposition to taking risks, because risk taking is all about the unknown.

Creative problem solving, a key skill for change agents, requires us to think of many solutions to the same problem. An equally important step is deciding on a potential solution and moving ahead with it. Therein lies the risk taking. At some point you must go from imagining what could be different to trying to make it happen. When you act on ideas about which you're not 100 percent certain, you're taking risks.

Obviously, you must be responsible in risk taking. Just because taking a risk is part of being a change agent doesn't mean that you do it just for the sake of doing it. Change agents take risks in the context of potential outcomes (both good and bad), weighing costs, benefits, and required resources. Responsible risk taking is possible and desirable.

Timing Is Everything

Another factor that affects change is timing. For change to be meaningful, it must be done well. This means that as a change agent you need to think through your reasons for change and your timing. Before you implement change, you need to consider questions such as these:

- Will people be available to help make the change happen?
- When will people most likely be receptive to this change?
- Do we have the resources available to make the change happen?

Even being a change agent for ourselves requires appropriate timing. In other words, we must consider whether now is the right time to make a given change. Would we be better served if we waited six months or a year?

Involving Others

Up to this point, the discussion about being a change agent has focused mostly on one person—you. Effective change agents, however, work with others to make change happen. Conversations with others enable a change agent to discover what can or should be done differently. Often change is effective only when you work with others. Although you may have come up with the original idea, you need others to help make the change occur and stick.

Let's go back to the example of running a meeting. Although you may be able to alter an agenda on your own, you need to work with others to develop the agenda so no one is caught off guard and everyone has a sense of what their new roles may be. Change developed or implemented in isolation generally results in turbulence, conflict, and sometimes rejection. You need others involved throughout the process: at the beginning, to help come up with what change would be valuable and develop a plan to make it happen; in the middle, to implement and troubleshoot; and at the end, to evaluate the change.

Conclusion

Being a change agent is easy for some and difficult for others. Are you looking for the possibilities of what's next, or are you content with what is? How you answer this question directly reflects your inclination toward change. Because change is all around us, the choice is yours. Which side of change do you want to be on: making it happen or waiting for it to happen to you?

Student Voice

"A leader must be present to guide and encourage, but to also set boundaries and rules, and be an enforcer."—*Male senior at*

University of Cincinnati, involved in a fraternity, honor society, professional organization, volunteer work, and a job/internship

---

"Change without leaders has much potential to be unorganized and temporary. Leadership creates unity, which is a must for change."—*Female sophomore at Appalachian State University, involved in a religious organization*

"For making change, I think that conflict is important, and by using methods of resolution, change becomes possible."—*Male sophomore at Florida State University, involved in a university programming board, residence hall association, volunteer work, and a job/internship*

Reflection Questions

- Think about how you tend to react to change. Write out your immediate gut reaction to how you feel about change.

- If you could have _____ any way you would like it to be, what would it look like? Fill in the blank with an area for change—a familiar context, setting, relationship, or a cause or an issue about which you feel passionately. Once you've filled in the blank, write your response to the question.

- Think through how you can begin to make any one of these changes happen. What are some important first steps? Who can help? When is the right time to initiate that change process?

19

CONFLICT MANAGEMENT

Identifying and Resolving Problems with Others

Effective leaders understand that conflict is part of any leadership experience, especially if change is involved. Conflict comes in many different shapes and forms. At times conflict is overt and may involve anger, raised voices, or high levels of frustration. Other times conflict is below the surface and shows itself only through cliques, side conversations, and apathy. Often conflict is a combination of all of these.

Harness the Potential in Conflict

Leaders with the ability to harness the potential energy inherent in conflict possess a wonderful skill. Emotionally intelligent leaders know that conflict can be a source of creativity and feedback. In many cases, working with or through conflict will yield an increased level of ownership for everyone involved. Based on this notion, we would like to underscore three concepts: (1) understanding the roots of conflict, (2) understanding how to work through conflict, and (3) hearing and responding to all voices.

The Roots of Conflict

Conflict arises for many different reasons; however, we have noticed a few common themes in our work with students: power struggles, conflicting values, member apathy, time, and leadership style.

- *Power struggles* arise in organizations when two or more individuals or groups seek to control the direction of the organization. You may have seen this occur during the course of the year or at a particular time (for example, during an election within your organization).

- Conflict might arise from a *difference in values or priorities*. For instance, different members or constituents may value different line items in the budget. Some prioritize one thing, others value another.

- Another source of conflict can be *apathy*. You may have seen or experienced what happens when some members or officers do very little and sit by while others do the majority of the work. This scenario can lead to resentment and conflict.

- *Time* can be another source of conflict. Some students have a lot of time to give whereas others do not. Similar to apathy, this can lead to factions and individuals on opposite sides of the fence.

- *Leadership style* is a perennial source of conflict. What kind of leader are you? Are you laid-back and easygoing or hard-driving and task-oriented? An individual who is a taskmaster may have problems leading a group of people who have a different style.

Work Through Conflict

When you experience conflict, be aware and try to work with it. Try not to get sucked in. If you can, try to stay uninvolved and watch the dynamics play out—doing so will place you in a better position than most to address the issues and help the group move through this very natural process. More often than not, a group

> You have to let everyone have their say in order to get them to cooperate and not just get angry and defensive.
> —*Female senior at University of Iowa, involved in a job/internship and as a peer writing tutor*

does not have an individual who can take on this role, and the conflict worsens because no one has perspective on the situation.

Understanding the process of moving a group through conflict is a challenge. The following specific actions can help a group through the process.

1. First, encourage the group to communicate in an open and honest manner. If need be, set some ground rules with which both sides can agree.

2. Next, ensure that all voices are heard. It is easy to get caught up in the conversation. You need to concentrate on being a facilitator so that all sides are heard.

3. In your own words, try to cut through the emotion and plainly summarize what you heard each side suggest as a course of action—minimizing and managing the emotions.

4. Finally, address any commonalities or shared ground between the two sides. For instance, both may want the same outcome but see different ways of arriving at a solution. Highlight commonalities and look for a third approach besides the two. Ask individuals to help focus on possibilities. If a third approach cannot be identified, explore other options, such as compromise.

> Always listen to everyone's ideas, because sometimes the most ridiculous-sounding idea ends up being the savior.
> —*Female senior at The Catholic University of America, involved in a residence hall association, job/internship, and orientation*

5. In the end, if you are unable to bring the two sides to consensus, you may need to either ask the larger group to vote or make a decision blending the two approaches. However, if you feel strongly that one course of action is the right and noble course, you may need to take a stand.

Conclusion

One point bears repeating: to resolve conflict effectively, all voices need to be heard. In the end, people need to feel that you care and have worked to provide them with a chance to share their perspective and be heard in the conversation. If they do not feel heard, they will not voice their opinions (at least not in the open). If they do not voice their opinions in the group, conversations go underground and you as a leader have a bigger problem on your hands. Conflict management is difficult; however, if the conflict is out in the open, everyone knows where everyone else stands. Emotionally intelligent leaders know this and use conflict management to benefit the group.

Student Voice

"Managing conflict means being agreeable, understanding, and willing to devote time and attention to generating alternatives and avenues for reaching those people that may be creating conflict. Managing conflict also means being willing to assume the negative feedback that may be concomitant with an environment where conflict exists."—*Male fifth-year senior at The Ohio State University, involved in a fraternity, student government, and a job/internship*

"You must utilize all of the resources of each member of the team. When a person has something to offer and feels that his/her assets are not being utilized, they will become disengaged. Conflict management works the same way. You must first acknowledge the mutual worth of each member, maintain a positive outlook, and acknowledge fault on both parts. At that point you can then start working toward a solution."—*Male junior at Miami University (Ohio), involved in a fraternity, honor society, student government, residence hall association, volunteer work, job/internship, and athletics*

Reflection Questions

- How do you normally confront conflict?
- How is conflict dealt with in your organization? In the open or underground? Effectively or not?
- How can you facilitate growth and development in your organization? How can you facilitate a culture of open and honest communication?

20

DEVELOPING RELATIONSHIPS

Creating Connections Between, Among, and with People

Developing relationships is as much a skill as a mindset. You are stronger, smarter, and more effective when you are in relationships with others. In fact, authorities on the topic of leadership have discussed the importance of relationships for years (Bass & Avolio, 1994; Blake & Mouton, 1978; Fiedler & Chemers, 1984; Graen & Uhl-Bien, 1995).

Some people assume you have to be outgoing or social to be effective at developing relationships. The truth is more complex than that. Many have discovered that the people who are best at developing relationships have a combination of skills and understanding that don't require them to be gregarious: they listen well, they know themselves well, they know how to develop rapport with others, and they understand the valuable role that others play in making their own life rich and fulfilling. So whether we are outgoing or shy, developing relationships is an essential life skill for us all. At the heart of this skill is the knowledge that you accomplish more when you engage with others and help others connect with one another.

Networking

Networking is one strategy for developing relationships. Networking means finding or making connections with others. It is an art, not a science. It is neither manipulative nor exploitative when done ethically and thoughtfully. Networking

- Increases your access to information
- Enhances your understanding of others

- Maximizes your effect on others
- Helps you develop meaningful relationships
- Improves your communication skills
- Builds credibility

A colleague who helps people find new jobs once said that networking is more about *who knows you* than whom you know. To make sure that others know you, you need to learn how to create or build your network of relationships.

Social Networks

To better understand your relationships, you can draw a "map" to see how you connect with others and identify how they connect with each other. Try this activity. Write your name in the middle of a blank sheet of paper, then write down the names of people with whom you come into contact frequently (friends, family members, associates) all around your name. Draw a line from your name to each of these names. Then, much like a connect-the-dot picture, draw lines between the people who know each other. Now add to the sheet the names of people whom these people know. Be sure to continue drawing the lines of connection as best you can. Don't forget to connect these additional people to you. Soon you may find that your page looks like a spider web. You now have a picture of your social network.

As you look at the map, think about your immediate connections and whether they are like you. Recent research demonstrates that the people you are closest to are generally quite like you, sharing common interests, values, and beliefs. This is called the self-similarity principle (Uzzi & Dunlap, 2005). As a result, although you may have relationships with many people, you don't often have relationships with many different kinds of people. This limits you. And it restricts your leadership potential.

Although it is comfortable and fun to spend time with people who are just like us, we become stifled if all we do is spend time with people who like and do the same things we do. Developing relationships in an emotionally intelligent way of diversifying our network. Engaging with people who are different from us allows us to learn about different ways of seeing the world and of doing things. Our leadership skills, problem-solving skills, ability to empathize with others, and creativity are all enhanced when we engage with people who are different from us.

Just Do It

The challenge of building a wide, diverse social network is the "how to." Here are a few thoughts on how to connect more with those around you.

Get Involved

It's hard to meet people when you stay at home most of the time or when you always do the same thing(s) with the same people. Developing relationships is about branching out. Get involved. Join a club. Volunteer. When someone sends you a generic invitation for an event, take them up on it. Participate. Woody Allen said, "Ninety percent of life is just showing up." And what better way to develop your leadership than to get more involved with others? You can learn many things from being exposed to different personalities, ideas, and styles of leadership, but you can see this only when you put yourself in a position to meet others. Remember, though, that balance is the key—you don't help anyone, including yourself, when you become overcommitted.

> Getting involved can do so much. Almost every relationship I have made thus far in college has been due to getting to know someone through initial contact or by getting involved.
> —*Male sophomore at Baldwin-Wallace College, involved in an honor society, residence hall association, professional organization, and athletics*

Connect with Connectors

In Malcolm Gladwell's ground-breaking book *The Tipping Point* (2000), he introduced the concept of connectors. Connectors are people who seem to know everyone. Although their relationships don't necessarily go deep, they go far and wide.

The good news is that you don't have to be a connector to get connected. Think through your network of friends, family, colleagues, and associates. Look back at your map. Who seems to have the most lines drawn to them? These people are likely connectors. Connect with them. Help them to get to know you better. Ask them whom they think you should get to know. Then follow up on their suggestions—make a phone call, write an email, call someone up for a cup of coffee. Whatever it takes, put yourself out there to have a conversation. Amazing things happen when people engage with one another.

Student Voice

"To build new relationships, I normally start by watching the person's interactions with other people. I want to know what they value in people and what their personal quirks are. Then I try to interact with them in a friendly manner and enjoy them. By understanding a person, spending time with them, and talking to them, I can build relationships."—*Female senior at MIT, involved in an honor society, volunteer work, job/internship, and a religious organization*

"Relationships are formed through trust and knowing the individual. You must be able to understand someone and relate to their situation."—*Male senior at University of Cincinnati, involved in a fraternity, honor society, professional organization, volunteer work, and a job/internship*

Reflection Questions

- Consider your network. Who has influenced your development and why? What do you get out of this relationship? To whom could that person introduce you to expand your network?

- About what area of your life do you want to know more? Who can help you get there?

- What do you do now to meet new people? What could you do differently?

21

TEAMWORK

Working Effectively with Others in a Group

Teamwork is needed in the classroom, the workplace, and virtually any organization. You may never have competed in a sport, yet you are expected to be a "team player." What does this mean? Is it just paying lip service to an ideal? Or is there really a way to work well with others? And does it matter? After all, isn't leadership really about results? Who cares how you get there as long as you get it done?

Leadership and Teamwork

Many definitions of leadership require teamwork, either explicitly or implicitly, as an essential skill. Consider these definitions:

- "Leadership is a process of persuasion and example by which an individual induces a group to take action." (Gardner, 1990)
- "A leader induces followers to act." (Burns, 1978)
- "Leadership is an influence relationship among leaders and followers." (Rost, 1991)
- "Leadership is a relational process of people together." (Komives, Lucas, & McMahon, 2007)

In each of these definitions, for leadership to occur the leader must work well with others. This is teamwork.

Teamwork is about developing and maintaining relationships. As an effective team player, you communicate well, especially on the listening end. You work to create respectful relationships. You cooperate with others.

Emotionally intelligent leadership involves knowing how to build a team and be a role model of collaboration. Effective leadership results in an environment in which working together is expected. Emotionally intelligent leaders know how to work with others to build a sense of group identity.

> Each person had to hold to their "section" of responsibility in order to accomplish the needs of the group as a whole.
> —*Female freshman at University of Wisconsin-Sheboygan*

When teamwork happens, people tap into their own potential and look for ways to contribute to the group. Members of a team intentionally invest time in other members of the team. As the team develops, members tap into their own talents without being asked. Team members grow as individuals when this occurs, and their contributions strengthen the organization at the same time.

The Challenge of Teamwork

The reality of group dynamics is that every collection of individuals does not become a team. Even official teams, sports teams for instance, are not always authentic teams. Teams have shared goals and shared understanding of purpose. When one member of the team operates with a hidden agenda, the team is nothing more than a group of people.

A true team must have a high level of trust. This takes time to build. Trust does not develop overnight, and it is easily lost. For trust to develop, team members must be honest with one another. Effective communication is an essential dynamic for a group if it is to develop into a team. Cooperation, collaboration, effective conflict management—all of these are in place when a team is operating at it highest level.

Conclusion

Teamwork implies togetherness. Cooperation and communication are essential. For instance, when you share helpful information without being asked, you are demonstrating teamwork. With the mantra "together we can do this better," you stay focused on what you can do to work well with others.

Student Voice

"In a group of eleven actors, we had thirty minutes to learn the entire last scene of a play. By encouraging them to study, rehearse, and play off of one another, coupled with the opening less than thirty minutes away, we memorized the last scene and it went off without a hitch. To work effectively, there must be initiative, dedication, efficiency, and guidance so as to be sure the goal is attained."—*Male junior at Baldwin-Wallace College, involved in the university programming board, student government, residence hall association, athletics, volunteer work, job/internship, and a religious organization*

"The real key to a successful team is having a firm understanding of the goal of the group, and then knowing how each individual can most effectively contribute to the achievement of this goal."—*Male senior at University of Nebraska–Lincoln, involved in a fraternity, honor society, religious organization, professional organization, job/internship, and volunteer work*

"For a team to succeed, people must be able to understand that each member has valuable input for the group. It is also important for the team not to come to decisions too quickly or too slowly. It is important to examine numerous possibilities to ensure that the action taken is one of the best options. A team must believe in each of its members and every member must contribute for a team to succeed."—*Female junior at The Catholic University of America, involved in an honor society, residence hall association, student government, athletics, volunteer work, and a religious organization*

Reflection Questions

- When have you been a member of a team? How did it feel?
- When is teamwork most important? When is it not needed?

22

CAPITALIZING ON DIFFERENCE

Building on Assets That Come from Differences with Others

Glory Road is a 2006 movie based on the true story of a college basketball team in the late 1960s. In his first year as the men's basketball coach at Texas Western University (TWU), Don Haskins decided that to have a championship-caliber team, he had to recruit a different type of player than the university traditionally had in the past. He sent his recruiters to Detroit, New York, and other northern cities to recruit African American men to play for TWU. In his first year of coaching, he succeeded in this recruiting effort and led his team to the NCAA national championship game with the first all-black starting line-up for a college basketball team.

Throughout the movie, the audience sees characters viewing the world based on their own assumptions, only to have those assumptions shattered by experience. The players held over from the previous year had to work with a first-year coach who had previously coached only a girl's high school basketball team. They didn't think this coach had anything to offer them. Some of these players had never met an African American. To find themselves on the same team caused some of the students to feel forced into an unwanted relationship. Confrontations and conflicts abounded.

One of the story lines in the movie is about how this diverse group of young men came together as a team. They overcame differences among themselves and with others outside the team. They learned how to build strength from their differences. The key factor was their ability to learn about each other, learn to appreciate each other, and create a shared understanding.

Assets, Not Barriers

Capitalizing on difference suggests that differences are seen as assets, not barriers. Difference may mean race, religion, sexual orientation, or gender as well as ability, personality, or philosophy. Whatever the difference, you have the capacity to learn about these differences. You can learn for understanding—that's one level. You can also go beyond understanding and learn to use differences to strengthen individuals and the group (or team). The challenge of difference lies in what you make of it.

> Different ideas are great because they offer different perspectives, but they can become a problem when no one is willing to accept differences.
>
> —Female junior at The Ohio State University involved in a sorority, athletics, volunteer work, and a job/internship

In *Glory Road*, one of the white players returns from summer break with the expectation of again being the star of the team. This young man knew nothing of the new coach or the new players. During the early practices, he assumed he would maintain his position as star; however, he discovered that the new coach did not share this assumption. Likewise, one of the African American men believed he had the talent and skills to be the star of the team. Conflicts arose among the players, between players and the coach, and eventually throughout the whole team.

Differences played out in relation to race, talent, and expectations. After a few confrontations, both physical and verbal, all team members realized that, in order to play basketball effectively as a team, they had to accept the reality that no one was leaving the team. The coach believed they could play together and that the team would be stronger for it. It took longer for the players to realize this than it did for the coach.

The two stars, and the team as a whole, stayed focused on their differences until people outside the team physically threatened and then assaulted different team members. When the team members realized that they were all being judged, they began to come together. They found common ground—primarily their desire to win. The two stars realized that they couldn't win without each other or the other players. Regardless of race, religion, or ability, everyone on the team wanted to be successful, and this became their shared understanding and goal.

During the NCAA tournament, the two stars played together better than ever. They had figured out a way to maximize their talents—building on their strengths and not worrying about their differences. The high point of the movie was when the coach announced that he would start an all-black line-up in the championship game. The young man who had been the star the previous year announced at this team meeting that he would cheer the hardest and loudest for the team. He was both courageous and inspirational with this announcement. He showed the whole team, himself, and the audience how rising above differences makes a difference.

Conclusion

Capitalizing on difference is a capacity that challenges each of us on a variety of levels. On one level, it may feel safest to "stick with" what or who we know, based on our similarities. Another challenge may be discovering that we may feel uncomfortable or even afraid when we are confronted by what sets us apart. This situation can result in us not sharing the best of what we have to offer. Capitalizing on difference, however, provides a different alternative; when we recognize our differences and search for ways to transform those differences into assets, we tap into unlimited potential.

Student Voice

"Leadership can easily be challenged by political/cultural/philosophical differences when it comes to work ethic or responsibility. They may feel that they do not have to go above and beyond the call of duty, and yet, if everyone else is doing it, they are expected to. Likewise, it can easily be an excuse to cause controversy or gain attention, which though inappropriate, is tricky to handle for fear of offending or disrespecting someone and their beliefs."—*Male junior at Baldwin-Wallace College, involved in the university programming board, student government, residence hall association, athletics, volunteer work, job/internship, and a religious organization*

"It is hard to be a leader when group members have cultural, philosophical, political, etc. differences."—*Female sophomore at Michigan Technological University, involved in orientation and a religious organization*

"It can be enhanced because differences can create a broader view and bring diverse opinions and backgrounds to the table. But, leadership can be challenged by these differences in that political, religious, philosophical and cultural views tend to be very strong and may not harmonize with those of others, causing conflict and doubt."—*Female freshman at University of Wisconsin-Sheboygan*

Reflection Questions

- What are the different facets of your identity? Write down all the different aspects of who you are according to some of the membership groups mentioned, such as race, religion, nationality, gender, and so forth.
- When are you with people who are most like you? What's it like?
- When are you with a broad mix of people? What is this like?

23

DEVELOPING EMOTIONALLY INTELLIGENT LEADERSHIP

A natural ending for a book on leadership is to provide some suggestions for practice. After all, it is natural for you to wonder about the next steps. In other words, how do you develop EIL? Here are a few suggestions.

A foundational concept of EIL is self-awareness, so this is a natural starting point. How do you increase your level of self-awareness? To put it succinctly, prepare yourself—because it takes a lot of hard work, and it is truly a lifelong journey.

Developing your self-awareness is an intentional process—like the development of any other knowledge, skill, or ability. As we've suggested previously, you learn more about yourself and thereby increase your self-awareness by seeking feedback from those who know you best. To do this, first ask yourself whether you are the type of person who naturally seeks feedback. Do you respond well to feedback? If the answer to this question is "maybe" or "no," then you know you have more work to do. Have courage and faith: the more you seek out feedback, the more you learn and the easier it gets. Try to become known as a person who is willing to accept and act upon the suggestions made by peers, mentors, and even family (if appropriate). Before you know it, you may receive feedback without asking for it—and more often than not this is a good thing.

Now that you are on the path to an increased level of self-awareness, you can begin to determine the capacities you hope to develop. For instance, you may discover (through feedback and personal reflection) that you demonstrate wonderful initiative, but acting as a change agent is hard for you. With this information in hand, you can begin to strategize the next steps.

The best way to improve your capacities is twofold. First, talk about it—let others know you want to improve and develop. By doing this, you will invite them to help you, and they can help hold you accountable to the actions you want to change or develop. They will also be in a better position to provide you with the much-needed feedback mentioned earlier.

Sharing with others that you want to improve yourself can be challenging because it places you in a vulnerable position. However, being in this state of vulnerability enables you to learn the most. When others know you're trying to learn something new, they tend to be more understanding of mistakes and perhaps more interested in helping you to learn. Think about how world-class athletes or musicians place themselves in the same position. To excel and develop their skills, they must be open to feedback.

Second, we suggest placing yourself in environments where you can practice the capacities you hope to develop. We call these *edge* experiences.

You know you are at your edge when you have a nervous feeling in your stomach—a feeling of uncertainty as to how things will turn out. For some, this may be public speaking; for others, it may be a deadline or a public leadership role. Being at the edge requires some risk taking.

What is your edge? What experience will take your abilities to a new level? Who can help you along the way? Clarity around these questions is paramount as you strive to develop your leadership capacities.

Before, during, and after a leadership experience, you must take time to reflect. Reflection takes many forms. For some, it is through writing or keeping a journal. For others, it is a conversation with a mentor, coach, teacher, or friend. Still others reflect while they exercise. Regardless of how you reflect, make sure you *do* reflect. One of the worst mistakes you can make in a leadership role is to focus solely on doing more and staying active. Skipping the reflection part is a huge loss to us all.

After all, it is in reflection that learning occurs. Think about it—football players do it when they watch tapes of their games and musicians do it when they listen to their recorded performances. These are all forms of reflection. Be sure to focus on how consciousness of context, consciousness of self, and consciousness of others play into your experience. Most important, take time to look at yourself in the mirror. As humans, we tend to externalize. In other words, we blame others when we fail. When you take time to reflect, you need to examine what you did well and what you did not do so well—that is, both your failures and your successes.

Another important aspect of your development is your environment. Place yourself in an environment with appropriate levels of challenge and support (McCauley & Van Velsor, 2005). Are the people in your environment helpful and, at the same time, able to challenge you? Or are they barriers to your overall development because they are either too supportive or too hard on you? Your environment is one of the most important and overlooked aspects of development. When you surround yourself with people who embody who you hope to become, you will have a better chance of becoming that person. The contrary is also true: a freshman who spends time with others known for partying will likely become a partier.

Finally, remember that you will never be finished with this work. This experience of enhancing your emotionally intelligent leadership will keep you in a constant state of investigation. The relationships among consciousness of context, consciousness of self, and consciousness of others are always changing. What works in one situation may not work in another. What was successful last week may not be successful next week.

So how do you know when to adjust your course? Often, you know you need to alter your strategies when things are too easy or too difficult. This means that if everything comes too easily, you're likely in a situation that is so comfortable that you're missing out on opportunities to grow and develop as a leader. Conversely, if you keep bumping up against challenge after challenge, never quite feeling that you're succeeding, then it is likely that the capacities you are currently demonstrating are not enough, or not well suited to get you where you hope to be. In either case, you may want to think about how to adjust course or develop a capacity that does not come naturally to improve your situation.

Conclusion

All of us are on a developmental journey, and all of us, at one time or another, will serve as leaders or followers. Some of us will monitor this process intentionally and some will not. This book is a guide to help you identify the critical capacities necessary for being an effective leader. Emotionally intelligent leadership is about combining your natural abilities with hard work. You have your own unique set of talents and capacities. And you have the potential to develop more. We wish you the best on your journey and hope you are successful in making your dreams, and the dreams of others, a reality.

References

Allen, K. E., & Cherrey, C. (2000). *Systemic leadership: Enriching the meaning of our work*. Lanham, MD: University Press of America.

Arvey, R. D., Rotundo, M., Johnson, W., & McGue, M. (2003, April). The determinants of leadership: The role of genetic, personality, and cognitive factors. Paper presented at the 18th Annual Conference of the Society of Industrial and Organizational Psychology, Orlando, FL.

Avolio, B., & Luthans, F. (2006). *The high impact leader*. New York: McGraw Hill.

Barker, J. (1991). *The power of vision* (VHS). United States: Starthrower Distribution.

Bar-On, R. (1997). *The Bar-On emotional quotient inventory (EQ-i): A test of emotional intelligence*. Toronto, Canada: Multi-Health Systems.

Bass, B. (1985). *Leadership and performance beyond expectations*. New York: The Free Press.

Bass, B. (1997). Does the transactional-transformational leadership paradigm transcend organizational and national boundaries? *American Psychologist, 52*(2), 130–139.

Bass, B., & Avolio, B. (1994). *Improving organization effectiveness through transformational leadership*. Thousand Oaks, CA: Sage.

Blake, R., & Mouton, J. (1978). *The new managerial grid*. Houston, TX: Gulf.

Blanchard, K. (1991). Situational view of leadership. *Executive Excellence, 8*(6), 22–23.

Blanchard, K., Zigarmi, P., & Zigarmi, D. (1985). *Leadership and the one minute manager*. New York: Morrow.

Burns, J. M. (1978). *Leadership*. New York: Harper & Row.

Caruso, D. (2003, October). Defining the inkblot called emotional intelligence. *Issues in Emotional Intelligence* (1). Retrieved February 20, 2004, from the Consortium for Research on Emotional Intelligence in Organizations website at http://www.eiconsortium.org

Collins, J. (2001). *Good to great: Why some companies make the leap and others don't*. New York: Harper Collins.

Conger, J. (1992). *Learning to lead: The art of transforming managers into leaders.* San Francisco: Jossey-Bass.

Covey, S. (1989). *Seven habits of highly effective people: Powerful lessons in personal change.* New York: Fireside.

Csikszentmihalyi, M. (1990). *Flow: The psychology of optimal experience.* New York: Harper & Row.

Driskill, G., & Brenton, A. L. (2005). *Organizational culture in action: A cultural analysis workbook.* Thousand Oaks, CA: Sage.

Fiedler, F. (1972). The effects of leadership training and experience: A contingency model interpretation. *Administrative Science Quarterly, 17*(4), 453–470.

Fiedler, F. E. (1996). Research on leadership selection and training: One view of the future. *Administrative Science Quarterly, 41,* 241–250.

Fiedler, F. E., & Chemers, M. (1984). *Improving leadership effectiveness: The leader match concept* (2nd ed.). New York: Wiley.

Gardner, H. (1999). *Intelligence reframed: Multiple intelligences for the 21st century.* New York: Basic Books.

Gardner, J. (1990). *On leadership.* New York: The Free Press.

Gladwell, M. (2000). *The tipping point: How little things can make a big difference.* New York: Little, Brown.

Goleman, D. (1995). *Emotional intelligence.* New York: Bantam Books.

Goleman, D. (1998). *Working with emotional intelligence.* New York: Bantam Books.

Goleman, D. (2000, March-April). Leadership that gets results. *Harvard Business Review.*

Goleman, D., Boyatzis, R., & McKee, A. (2002). *Primal leadership: Realizing the power of emotional intelligence.* Boston, MA: Harvard Business School Press.

Graen, G. B., & Uhl-Bien, M. (1995). Relationship-based approach to leadership: Development of leader-member exchange (LMX) theory of leadership over 25 years: Applying a multi-level multi-domain perspective. *Leadership Quarterly, 6*(2), 219–247.

Heifetz, R. A. (1994). *Leadership without easy answers.* Cambridge, MA: Belknap Press of Harvard University Press.

Heifetz, R. A., & Linsky, M. (2002). *Leadership on the line.* Cambridge, MA: Harvard Business School Press.

Higher Education Research Institute. (1996). *A social change model of leadership development: Guidebook version III.* Los Angeles: University of California Los Angeles Higher Education Research Institute.

Hunt, J. G. (1991). *Leadership: A new synthesis.* Thousand Oaks, CA: Sage.

The International Coach Federation. Retrieved May 4, 2006, from www.coachfederation.com

Jaworski, J., & Flowers, B. S. (1998). *Synchronicity: The inner path of leadership*. San Francisco: Berrett-Koehler.

Komives, S. R., Longerbeam, S., Owen, J. E., Mainella, F. C., & Osteen, L. (2006). A leadership identity development model: Applications from a grounded theory. *Journal of College Student Development, 47*, 401–420.

Komives, S. R., Lucas, N., & McMahon, T. R. (2007). *Exploring leadership: For college students who want to make a difference* (2nd ed.). San Francisco: Jossey-Bass.

Kouzes, J. M., & Posner, B. Z. (2007). *The leadership challenge: How to get extraordinary things done in organizations*. San Francisco: Jossey-Bass.

McCauley, C. D., & Van Velsor, E. (Eds.). (2005). *The center for creative leadership handbook of leadership development*. San Francisco: Jossey-Bass.

Northouse, P. (2002). *Leadership: Theory and practice* (2nd ed.). Thousand Oaks, CA: Sage.

Rost, J. (1993). *Leadership for the 21st century*. Westport, CT: Praeger.

Salovey, P., & Mayer, J. D. (1990). Emotional intelligence. *Imagination, Cognition, and Personality, 9*(3), 185–211.

Segal, J. (1997). *Raising your emotional intelligence: A practical guide*. New York: Henry Holt.

Uzzi, B., and Dunlap, S. (2005). How to build your network. *Harvard Business Review, 83*(12), 53–60.

Weisinger, H. (1998). *Emotional intelligence at work*. San Francisco: Jossey-Bass.

When executive coaching fails to deliver. (2003). *Training Strategies for Tomorrow, 17*(2), 17.

Williams, C. (2005). *Management* (3rd ed.). Mason, OH: South-Western College Publishing.

Yukl, G. (2002). *Leadership in organizations* (5th ed.). Upper Saddle River, NJ: Prentice Hall.

Index